YES, NO, OR NOT YET

— a novel —

SARA LIVELI

Yes, No, or Not Yet

Trilogy Christian Publishers
A Wholly Owned Subsidiary of Trinity Broadcasting Network
2442 Michelle Drive, Tustin, CA 92780

Copyright © 2025 by Sara Liveli

All Scripture quotations, unless otherwise noted, are taken from THE HOLY BIBLE, NEW INTERNATIONAL VERSION®, NIV® Copyright © 1973, 1978, 1984, 2011 by Biblica, Inc.® Used by permission. All rights reserved worldwide.

All rights reserved, including the right to reproduce this book or portions thereof in any form whatsoever. For information, address Trilogy Christian Publishing Rights Department, 2442 Michelle Drive, Tustin, CA 92780.

Trilogy Christian Publishing/ TBN and colophon are trademarks of Trinity Broadcasting Network.

For information about special discounts for bulk purchases, please contact Trilogy Christian Publishing.

Trilogy Disclaimer: The views and content expressed in this book are those of the author and may not necessarily reflect the views and doctrine of Trilogy Christian Publishing or the Trinity Broadcasting Network.

10 9 8 7 6 5 4 3 2 1
Library of Congress Cataloging-in-Publication Data is available.

ISBN 979-8-89597-026-3
ISBN 979-8-89597-027-0 (eBook)

DEDICATION

I want to dedicate this book to you, the reader. Wherever you are in your life's journey, please know you are one courageous person to face the hard parts of life, especially in crisis. May you ask for help and continue to be a lifelong learner. When you know better, you do better.

I want to thank all those who have shown their love, support, and continuous wisdom to me all these years. My family would not be where it is today without your intentional care and candor. Words cannot express how grateful I am. Thank you.

We only have the present day each day to live and can choose to make the most of it or not.

Betrayal comes from those we deeply love. When it hurts so much, it is because we loved so much, and I submit to you that is how it should be. And yet, it is the very thing I have said multiple times: "It is not supposed to be that way." Husbands and fathers are not supposed to be cowards and leave their vows and children. Yet, betrayal showed me how genuinely I loved.

My home church pastor said it best, "They are responsible for their sin, and we are responsible for our bitterness." We are presented the choice once again: choose healing and freedom or bitterness, which causes rottenness in the bones. Do the right thing and God can help you.

Even when I truly can say I tried to do the right thing with the plethora of decisions I faced and am still facing, it still did not mean it did not hurt. It hurts because a prayer I have prayed for years through this season is "Lord, keep my heart tender." God has answered that prayer, and that tenderness allows me to grieve those that I love even though that is not who is in front of me now.

I want this book to address this very paradox of grieving the living and having peace that only comes from heaven to guide us. We can see our loved ones right there in front of us, yet it is so different.

PREFACE

Who truly wants to write about one of the most painful parts of their life's experience? I've been doing the healing work these past many years and thought it was good. I have laid it to rest. Yet tonight I realize that my story is not just for myself. There are too many families dissolving in our present world. There are too many sheltered Christian young wives going into marriages that have no idea what the signs are and keep giving the benefit of the doubt over and over to "honor their husbands," even while riding the waves of dishonor for far too long, and then the worst thing gets revealed. But it is far worse than anything she could ever have imagined. Especially in my situation—a little under six weeks away from having our second child and being in the most vulnerable state a woman can be in when the carpet is ripped out from under you.

    I will be coming from my background as a Christ follower. I grew up in the church but was thankful to be the first generation in my family to have known God from a young age. My faith in God, Jesus, and the Holy Spirit, along with the support and kindness of those who graciously walked this path of unknowns, grief, pain, anger, doubts, and love is what got me and my family through each day. I cannot imagine going through such huge moments of loss in this life and not having a relationship with our Creator. I hope my story is one that can bring you hope, restore your faith that there is beauty in each day, and enable you to still love and show love while working through the sorrow and pain.

We were taught way too many things from Scripture that our human selfishness twisted to the "modern day" Christian wife when really God's original design was the man and woman in partnership side by side, and it was not until the Fall, when sin entered the world in the Garden of Eden, that man was then placed over the woman. Yet didn't Jesus redeem us back to that after He died and rose again on the Cross? Why haven't our own home churches embraced the beauty of the woman in marriages? The Holy Spirit is also known as the helper and is made no less.

I argue that if we truly believe Jesus redeemed all of it, then give the respect and honor to us women, wives, mothers, and friends. Now this book is not one for political standing (who knows, maybe that will be a sequel). This book is one for those caught in crisis and not sure what each moment or day will bring. I want to share my story, as I did not go through all of this to not help others. I also think it's ironic to write it in a book, as when you're in crisis the last thing you have time for is to read a book. I'm hoping one day to make it short clips, as I remember I could read captions on videos each morning as I nursed our new son while in the middle of a cross-country move, taking care of our three-and-a-half-year-old at the time and a husband completely in shambles. We had no income, as he lost his job and rightfully so.

We had put all of our savings into the house we had finished flipping and were presently living in. I had one month's worth of savings that would cover the month of March, and then nothing after that, and I was to then give birth two weeks later. The last place I wanted to live in was our home, knowing what all had happened in it without my knowledge. And yet, where was I to go as I was bringing new life to our home—a home that was literally nothing I thought it would be? And the last place I wanted to stay was in that city where this all happened.

That helped keep my perspective broad, and also that was all the time I had and bandwidth as well. It's time to write my story. I write it for my children to know and understand that life is tough, but it is one that we do not have to walk alone, as Jesus is right there with us. I write it for men and women so that if some part of my story can help them navigate this beautiful gift of life even during painful seasons for themselves or someone they know, then so be it.

I am writing it coming from the background that I dated my high school sweetheart, even though we went to two different high schools and met in our sister youth group activities. We had dated for four years, were engaged for one year, and then we married at twenty-one years old. We both came into our marriage as virgins and entered a monogamous relationship. These were our core values and boundaries, and I share that so as you are reading this book, it will help give you the perspective as to why this type of betrayal was so hurtful for our family. *Yet, one of the most amazing gifts God has given us is free will and the ability to choose.* For our marriage, these were the pillars of what we chose for our relationship, and then for one party to exercise their own free will in that manner left a huge trauma wake. I want to share my story to give the practical and spiritual elements, as well as to share how to lead through its points of conflict for you as the reader.

I also want to say there is way too much shame wrapped around divorce or separations because that can be the most courageous act a person may need to take, rather than stay in a very unhealthy relationship. I come from a background where staying in marriage for the long haul is the goal no matter what boundaries another crosses. That is anything but what God called us to do here on earth. Marriage is a daily choice of love. Love being defined as laying down one's life for another. A completely selfless act. So, what do you do when the polar opposite happens in your marriage? When your spouse decides to continue in the most selfish decisions?

Trust is broken, and the gates have to go up and new boundaries must be redrawn until trust is built again. This may look like speaking with a lawyer ASAP to understand how to stop the bleeding financially, mentally, and emotionally. This may need to look like restraining orders, new bank accounts, new living situations temporarily, or changing the locks on the doors. Many will not make it back from the initial blow, much less some form of a new relationship. I had heard how it can be sweeter than it was before. I truly wanted that to be us and my family as a whole, but sadly, where we sit today, that is still not our present reality even many years later. There have been moments of that, and I am thankful for those, but now I know those were called breadcrumbs, as the lack of consistency shows otherwise. *Words spoken without the changed behavior to back it up is manipulation, not hope.*

In spite of all of these things, one thing remains true, and that is my faith in Jesus. I am not sure how others go through such hard things in life without leaning on their faith in their Creator. One of the greatest things this world can testify to is that God the Father, a supreme being, sent His Son Jesus to earth in order to reconcile this world back to Him that we may have eternal life in heaven. Until heaven comes, our purpose on this earth is to know Jesus, listen to His leadings, and share Christ with others. I write this for my sons to know that even through life's hardships, we must still choose love. God is love. Turn towards your Creator and not away, as it is His love that will sustain you each day. That is it. Love well, my dearest sons, because you are so loved by me and your Heavenly Father, more than you could ever know in this lifetime.

INTRODUCTION

Who wants to read a book on endurance? When you're in the midst of an enduring situation, you just want relief. A moment, a second to feel normal again. To feel like your world and your children's world is safe. That is one of life's greatest lessons: *that we cannot control others.* We are accountable for our own actions and how we treat people. The greatest tool we have is our relationship with Jesus. Your situation and mine is not new to Him. He has seen all of this under the sun a thousand times, yet He is with us in our pain. He is with us to endure. There comes a time to realize we are not our own gods. We may think we are and we may be "living up sin" like there is no tomorrow. And grant it, if you're doing sin well, it is fun. It also has a lot of consequences. Consequences that not only affect you, the person making those decisions, but everyone else around you as well.

We are not called to live a perfect life. That is a lie, and please do not get caught missing your life because you think you can be perfect and yet it will never be attainable. What a waste of time and energy. We are called to know and see our imperfections, and that is why it is so important to rely on Jesus and listen to the voice of the Holy Spirit. The wisdom of this world ends right there, at this world. The wisdom of the heavenly places is far beyond what we can comprehend. That is where faith comes into play. If we could plan our lives all out and know the outcomes to make better decisions, then that would not be faith. That is logic or reason. I argue that we need both: logic and faith.

In saying all of that, I hope my story I share with you can remind you to keep your eyes on Jesus each day, whether in crisis or good times. He holds your world in His hands if you let Him. There is no better place to be than in our Savior's arms, just as we are.

CONTENTS

Dedication iii
Preface v
Introduction xi

Chapter 1: This Is My Story 15
Chapter 2: Unscented 45
Chapter 3: Relaxing Lavender 51
Chapter 4: Wild Vanilla 53
Chapter 5: Pine Scrub 57
Chapter 6: Orange Citrus 59
Chapter 7: Cedarwood Spice 61
Chapter 8: Sweet Honeysuckle 63
Chapter 9: Peppermint Eucalyptus 69
Chapter 10: Pumpkin Spice 71
Chapter 11: Espresso Delight 73
Chapter 12: Soothing Sandalwood 77
Chapter 13: The City Blend 79
Chapter 14: Crisp Evergreen 81
Chapter 15: Closing Chapter 85
Chapter 16: The Unknown 105

CHAPTER 1

This Is My Story

This is my story: betrayal, broken-hearted, fatherless, abandoned, destitute, pregnant, penniless, jobless, mocked, rejected, the last one standing.

In one week, I lost my husband and my home; he lost his job; I was betrayed by my spouse; my best friend was gone; I was rejected by family; and I was 35 weeks pregnant.

One night while folding laundry, my husband walks into our bedroom, cold as ever, and could not even get the words out. I had to ask so many questions to find out that he was leaving with another woman. It was as if the truth that finally came out after a yearlong affair hit him, and tears came down his face as he ran out of the house. It was not a confession but rather a notification. No remorse. He was leaving me and going off to marry his mistress and live in the city next to ours was all that he could get out before running out of the house.

I waddled myself off the edge of our bed in shock to the kitchen where he had gone through out to the garage, only to find a note on the kitchen counter ripped from some leftover mail with two words written on it: "I'm sorry." In this moment and still for six months more to come, I had no idea the full story behind those two words. What exactly was he sorry for? Where did he just leave to go, and was he ever coming back?

I never imagined I would have to face this reality. The shock took my breath away, as this was a time in our lives when money was good, he was promoted at work, we bought our next home and renovated it, baby was on the way, and our sex life was on point. I was thankful for a smooth pregnancy with our second child. I was in the middle of getting my graduate degree and enjoying California life, staying home, still raising our son. I was even watching my niece a few times a week and other times some other friends' kiddos. Life was sweet, right?

The major red flag that stood out this whole time was the breakdown in our communication and him constantly being on his phone via text or whatever messaging was occurring. That was not uncommon with the job he had, and typically when I asked him to put it down, I was met with the answer, "It's work, and I have to answer." I tried every which way to find peace with him in our home. It was not happening on our own, and I finally said we must get help, especially before the baby comes. I finally got him to agree to go to couples counseling, and for the next three months prior to the baby's due date, we were in couples counseling weekly, and the therapists never uncovered an affair. He was a master with words, maintaining his image; now I know it is called gaslighting and flipping stories on to me as if I were the one lying or being unfaithful. None of which could be further from the truth. *What I learned now is that projection was a backwards way of him "confessing" what he was doing that was not acceptable to our relationship.*

Never in my wildest dreams did I ever think this would happen in our relationship. All those dreams, visions of how our precious unborn baby boy would be brought into this world were gone. Everything was stripped away. My security, and in the weeks to follow, my dignity as well. The two main places where I felt I lost my dignity, even though that was the last thing I had lost, were the follow-up appointment in my ob-gyn office and going to the welfare office.

When this crisis fully revealed itself, it was what it was. I could not change his decisions. I did not even know what the next moment, much less the next day, would look like. What was left and will always remain is Jesus. He is my security, and everything else bows at the name of Jesus. I am thankful that each day before life hit the fan, I learned to pray, to walk in love, and by God's grace, to see my spouse and life as Jesus sees it. He is and always will be faithful. He will be found when we seek His face.

I had a choice in that moment of betrayal and many more to come to walk in faith and allow God's grace and mercy to flow through my actions or allow fear, anger, and self-righteousness to cloud my vision.

The vision being that I am the last one standing for my immediate family. And by God's strength, I knelt to the floor and reminded God of my covenant with Him and my covenant of marriage between my husband, me, and Jesus. Steve couldn't see it and wouldn't for some time to come, if ever, but all authority had been given to Jesus in heaven and on earth. And it's in Jesus' name that I prayed and said amen with tears streaming down my face. The ironic part is I did not need to remind God. He knows. It was a moment of faith for me.

I got up and set my face as flint to bring Steve home. (However, Sara, many years out from all of this, wants to interject and remind you that God has given each person their own free will. In that free will, we are only responsible for our own actions. What we enable, accept, or even encourage is our part. Our own needs are just as important and even more important during crises or big life changes.) Each day I prayed, *Lord, help my unbelief,* and He did.

Jesus met my needs even before I knew I had them. Those first few days felt like weeks or even months, as it wasn't about the affair but about Steve being alive the next day. For Steve to know Christ and His grace, for Steve to see his children grow up and to be restored to his wife. Yet, in crisis, remember you have to focus on your own needs, and you are responsible for your own actions.

Then, I went into survival mode. This bomb just went off in our personal life. Steve was getting the help he needed (we flew him to Colorado for intensive therapy), and now my priority was my own health and to bring our unborn son into this world safely. To take care of myself, our three-and-a-half-year-old son, and our unborn child. I have never felt so alone and in the wilderness and yet so at peace. A peace that only Christ can give you.

At this point, the priority was knowing that Steve was in intensive therapy out of state and had lost his job, and rightfully so. This all happened within the first four days of Steve running out of our house. However, that meant at 35 weeks pregnant, how do I even live and provide for my own family? Who is going to hire a 35-week pregnant woman? Much less a pregnant lady whose life just went up in flames. My biggest piece of advice is to take it in chunks. Call in support from a trusted mentor. Someone who can help you think objectively in a crisis.

At this point in time, the marriage is going to have to be on hold. As frustrating and messy as our now-revealed relationship was, that had to wait. I had to figure out how to bring our unborn child into this world safely. I had to figure out the money and how I was going to support my family and then go from there, and by the way, I had less than four weeks to figure out the money piece before giving birth. Hopefully, I even had four weeks without the stress triggering me into preterm labor. How can we live? Can we stay in this home? Do we even stay in this home? So many questions swirled in my mind. First things first, I needed to check on my physical health and take it from there.

Nothing can prepare you to call your ob-gyn office and have to schedule an emergency appointment with the nurse and them ask for the reason, especially when Steve came with me to every appointment, but not this one. I could barely get the words out because the shock was so fresh, and yet I had to know the health of my own body and figure out what kind of birth I could have so as not to pass anything on to our unborn son. I sat in the doctor's office getting tested for sexually transmitted diseases, unable to answer basic questions because my own husband had a whole other life going on. (Thankfully, the results showed I did still have a clean bill of health, and I know this is a miracle considering the things they engaged in.)

I also remember walking into the welfare office and being given a number and treated like one too. It is a place no one should have to turn to, and yet there I was. Where were all the church leaders, Christian university leaders that knew the position I was now in, family, extended family I looked up to leading or covering me in this manner? Why is it that at the end of the day, I had to turn to a government system for help when I am an educated woman, getting my master's degree? I have family on both sides, am well connected socially, my character is intact and always has been, and yet I was given a number. My child and unborn child given a number by the state. It should not be this way for anyone.

When it comes to money, I learned through this time in my life that money exposes the true character of a person. It exposes what is already there. It either shows more selfishness or shows some of the most generous people. For those who showed the latter, whether financially or with your time or talent, I truly thank you. I thank you for all the meals, childcare, hospital rides for delivery, selling our home, airport rides, packing up the house, moving across the country, and so much more. Thank you for your kindness.

Our home went on the market, and nineteen showings later, after three offers and inspections, it sold. Then, on June 8, we closed, and at eight weeks postpartum, I flew to Colorado with my sons to face Steve for the first time in weeks and to deal with the affair head-on.

I knew he didn't hold to his word to break it off with his mistress like he told me. But in all actuality, he never ended it and kept keeping on with her. Mind you, she was also married, and my husband, Steve, knew her husband presently, since we went on a mission trip together back in our college days. Steve's mistress was also his employee at work, and we all attended the same church together as well. Her husband was also on staff at our home church. She even attended the baby shower that my sister-in-law threw for me just three weeks prior to when Steve walked out. This shows the amount of blatant disrespect and how, when one engages in sexual immorality, they open themselves up to spiritual confusion. When Scripture says "the heart is deceitful and beauty is vain, but one who fears the Lord will be saved," I could not concur more. The heart is deceitful. "We're soulmates!" Umm, no, you're not. Steve is married and you are married. What you two are doing is deceiving one another to think that even your guy's relationship could ever last the haul when built on lies and deception. There is no trust between the deviated relationship and now your current spouses.

When the truth finally was revealed, this hit in every area of our lives: home, children, family, work, church, friend social circles, and so forth. I could not even go to the grocery store without someone coming up to me who knew about it. Yet I was not saying anything on social media or texting folks. Word spread like wildfire, and the number of times people thought it was okay to just show up at my house or walk in the front door without asking was astonishing.

Please know that when this happens in your relationship, it is now your responsibility to lead your family. It is your life, your children, your wayward husband, and you are now the decision-maker. "They" can either support you and follow your lead, but it is never acceptable for another family member, especially another male family member, to think they are now going to be "your temporary husband." It is my family, and it is my call. That was another wave of stress—the initial fall out of close extended family processing through the affair being revealed. Sadly, some of those family members knew about the affair six months prior to Steve telling me. (This all was revealed four months after having our second son when we were now living in Colorado.) They confronted Steve about it those six months before he walked out. He denied anything was going on, and then they continued to keep their mouths shut even when I brought to their attention that we as a couple needed help, and I was trying to get Steve to go to couples therapy with me. The betrayal was not only with my husband but also now with close extended family members that lived near us in California.

Once our new baby boy was born, the house finally closed, and I got cleared postpartum to fly. My dear friend flew with me and our two boys to Colorado and it was time for the next chapter. To get to this point, I had six close friends of mine running different aspects of my daily life. It took a whole team for four months straight and thousands of decisions to get to this point. Yet God was in all the details each and every day. God uses people. Us, the body of Christ, strangers, whoever is willing. These six ladies were willing and always followed through. I am forever grateful for their faithfulness.

- Friend #1 — coordinated groceries and meals for me, anything for the physical needs to be met.
- Friend #2 — took weekly walks to help with the contractions and was there mentally/emotionally for me. She helped with anything regarding the hospital and baby (took me to the hospital for labor and delivery four times, and then because

I knew Steve would fly back for the birth, my body then would reverse and contractions would still happen nonstop for two weeks). Post-birth, she came to my home as I was bent over in pain and took me to the ER. (Thankfully, it was a UTI and all cleared, but so many layers of stress.)
- Friend #3 — provided childcare weekly for our older son. I would always put our older son down for naps or bedtime and play after dinner some, as I did not want to have our older son lose both parents at the same time. I am forever grateful for friend #3, as I could not have done that without her, and especially with a newborn too for part of that time as well.
- Friend #4 — She was my right hand. Her wisdom, prayers, humor, and do-whatever-it-takes attitude sustained me. She also confronted others graciously, even when they meant well but the execution or timing was not appropriate.
- Friend #5 & #6 — drove me to all the hard meetings, i.e. workplaces, school, banking, lawyer offices, welfare office, real estate closing meetings, and to the airport to leave a life I once knew behind.

Then, I would text others to help coordinate the move, selling items, cleaning the house for showings, babysitting, and the list went on and on. These ladies had families, jobs, husbands, and children of their own. They somehow figured out how to have their own homes be held down in order to hold down what was left of mine. I knew their husbands stepped up a lot to hold down their own homes, and because I could see that from a distance, it kept my faith in men.

One of the most healing moments for me happened one Sunday morning when my friend and her husband invited me to their church. We had not even made it inside when my older son, who was still a toddler, ran off across this field in front of their church. I was still pregnant and in no way able to run after him. My son had so many changes and new faces in front of him in such a short amount of time that he was a bit overwhelmed. My friend's husband showed such godly kindness to my son by just sitting with him out in that field, and his wife then sitting with me on the front stoop of the church, was the most Christ-like moment my whole family needed. They just knew how to sit with someone and be. Not push an agenda, pressure to get into the building. *They met us where our capacity was in that moment.*

California was now wrapped up logistically, even though every day the layer of emotional chaos between Steve and I was constant. I had to lean on my therapist as to how to navigate that unhealthy communication from Steve, even in the midst of the present trouble. (I highly recommend finding a therapist that can walk you through a crisis. It is too much to do alone, and we are not supposed to.) My friend, my children, and I flew to Colorado. I pulled up to a townhome that friends of ours helped find for us. They cleaned and coordinated the move-in day as well. Even in the "getting settled" again in a new home, a new state, and a new place in life, the emotional chaos was still present in our marriage.

I redrew the lines with Steve. I asked him to have some respect that until we are 100 percent one way or the other, all the lies, games, phone calls, and emails with his mistress end now. If he's so proud of his relationship, then no more secrets. He wants to call her or text her, then do it. Not this secrecy of profiles and whatever else. Welcome to real life. He wants to keep throwing out the word divorce. Then I'm going to be informed and know what that actually means. I met with a divorce lawyer in Colorado and everything recommended to me was to file for maintenance of separation while we were in the in-between time. I kept feeling like the Spirit told me to wait. *Wait on Me and know that I am your provider, as he has been.* So, I waited.

One night, after being up in our new rental townhome in Colorado for a few weeks, Steve told me he made his choice and it was her. It broke my heart all over again, but that peace rested on my shoulders. I knew it would be okay. I didn't know how, but that's faith. And again, he was in the fetal position under the counter in the kitchen.

I will not live in fear, I kept reminding myself. *Lord, give me faith to trust You and not the circumstances in front of me.* Not taking offense, even when it's completely justified because you know he doesn't know what he's doing. (Technically, he did, but his filter wasn't on right.)

I also have to interject and say there were a host of close people, family, friends, counselors, and pastors that helped me navigate moments, hours, and days. I will say I had to do my part and ask for help. Reach out to those I knew I could trust.

Be okay with knowing that not everyone may step up or can help. Those that did, if you're reading this, thank you. It literally was and still is the greatest gift, showing up with selfless love in someone else's crisis. You prayed with me, held my arms up like Aaron did with Moses, held our older son in your arms, and the gift of life, a new baby boy, in your arms too. Some may never understand this, but the times when this close circle of support hugged me, it was truly healing, as in a crisis there are few moments of touch or love toward the primary caregiver when a family is falling apart. I thank you from the bottom of my heart.

Those that led with integrity and showed mercy, I thank you. When you thought you were showing mercy to Steve, you were actually showing me and the kids mercy too, for our lives to not take on more hardship than what was already given. I thank you for seeing the bigger picture, and I recognize your kindness as strength and not weakness. Many decisions that I had to make were misunderstood and some also took my kindness as weakness. Here is the thing: I learned that it is okay to be misunderstood. *Make the best and most informed decisions you can and go from there.*

Practical Applications in My Story

We had been in couples counseling from January 2017 through March 2017. I did not realize, nor did our counselor sniff out, how he had lied his way through those months of counseling. I had asked to go with him to counseling because the breakdown in how he was communicating with me had to end. It especially needed to get back on track before our second baby would be born. *I say do not give up on fighting for your own needs, even when it does not turn out how you hoped.*

I would also say it is not okay for anyone to continuously speak to you disrespectfully. Looking back, the worse he spoke to me at home, the further he was going in breaking our marriage vows. I kept thinking it was for this reason or that. He's stressed at work, or the renovation of our home is bothering him, and on and on. I kept giving him the benefit of the doubt because I never imagined anything like this could have happened between us. I would confront him on it, and he always had some sort of reason, and yet no apology would come or, if it did, the apology would be with an irritated tone. There is no reason for anyone to constantly or even for a moment be disrespectful in words or boundaries, and even after you bring it to their attention, there is no change of action.

Furthermore, get informed. I knew where all our financial papers were and had access to all those documents as well before this crisis hit. He traveled domestically and internationally quite often, and this was us being responsible in case something would happen, but never an affair and him leaving with another person all in the same breath. *I would highly encourage each couple to both get on the same page of where all the different paperwork is in case of a crisis and not after the fact.*

Lastly, get informed by a lawyer. I was not making any rash decisions in that state of crisis, but I also was not going to be blindsided anymore either and needed to put in practical buffers. I had our children to protect. The best way to protect our children and whatever type of relationship Steve and I would have was to be informed. Get educated! You do the right thing even when others will not. Remember to keep your own integrity even when others lack self-control.

The Reality of Consequences

I share this next part not in a condemning way, but know that when you violate trust in a monogamous marriage relationship, there will be consequences. I hope in sharing these it can serve as a reality check for some and also a warning for others. At any point in time over that year to year and a half, Steve could have made the decision to stop. It typically starts off small, with compromising boundaries. Then, that snowball can keep growing and growing if you let it. Once again, we can exercise the gift of free will for good or evil at any point in any area of our lives. This is also why we cannot be our own gods because then the lines for what we want for us and our best interests are constantly changing. This arbitrarily violates others' boundaries around you. I would even argue that there is no decision that solely impacts you. The belief in a Higher Power or Being is the one thing that can bring order to a chaotic heart or spirit. Jesus is our moral compass, and He set the example way before that day.

These were the consequences of his actions that affected me, our children, and so many others. I listed them not for shame purposes, but so others will know it is not worth it as it causes a trail of pain. Pain that some may never comeback from. I know it was miraculous for me in more ways than one.

- He left me with all the bills to pay and I had no job. (There was our home, the birth of our second son, his medical bills, cars, etc.)
- Our kids were impacted and the world flipped upside down from one day to the next.
- Bringing our baby boy into this world was not how I thought that would look in any way, shape, or form.
- There was the main betrayal and then the continuation of betrayal after he told me about the affair. I was having to entertain that the mistress was here again and she'd watch my children! Laws do not protect a mother in my position. I just lost my husband, and now I may have to share our kids with the same individuals that broke our family apart? They put our kids' worlds into more turmoil because they did not just lose a father but also their last constant force as their mom. Our kids growing up in a broken home (rotating weekends and the stress of more changes). Having to find a job ASAP and kids go to daycare (that was a family value to raise them at home as littles), yet who would hire a third trimester pregnant lady? All sense of security was gone.
- Medical bills.
- Graduate school gone—this was a perk of his job—my graduate school was covered, and I only had five classes left, but that was gone. I had to withdraw from the program for many

reasons. I was living like a single mom, even though I was married.
- Praying for our oldest son through his night terrors. (His stress was coming out in his sleep.)
- Dry pumping and screaming through contractions to help induce labor naturally but to no avail. I was in triage four times; I would get checked in and the contractions would stop once I was at the hospital because it was a trigger for me that I'd see Steve soon. (He would fly back in for the birth each time to California and then fly back out to Colorado because he was in therapy and looking for a new job in Colorado.)
- Active labor for ten days with no relief and constant contractions no less than 8–10 minutes apart—then the induction.
- ER visit with severe abdominal pain (UTI) after birth and dragged myself to the front door to let a friend in while the new baby boy screamed on the bed.
- Getting tested for HIV and STDs while being pregnant, as his actions put my health and our unborn child's health at risk.
- Feeling so isolated and rejected. (I had six amazing women walk this journey with me, and I am forever grateful.)
- Completely blindsided, and everything that was happening to me was out of my control. None of it was because of my decisions, and there I was to face it and deal with the consequences.

- Dealing with my milk coming in and the supply issues. Dealing with formula and the cost that came with that, as well as what type of formula my baby boy could tolerate.
- Moving into a townhome that I had never seen in person, and even with the profit from the sale of our home in California, I still almost lost the townhome without a cosigner who had a job. Once again, a sense of security was not fully mine.
- Loss of a partner and spouse.
- Comparisons and *what if* mind games.
- Packing and the constant daily logistics and life logistics. All Steve had to do was find a job in Colorado and go to work, and he had all the free time at night at a friend's home he stayed at in Colorado. Well, I hope you used your time wisely (which he didn't by still engaging with his mistress), because when me and the kids get up to Colorado, it's go time. Side note: Ladies, Jesus did not die for you to be used by men, and especially not married men and you being a married woman as well. God never wants us to be mistreated, much less ongoing mistreatment that is called abuse.
- Being questioned by both families and given all their opinions, but their opinions were about what they thought was best for me when it was really about what's best for them. It came from a good place, but they did not have the emotional

capacity to navigate this next beginning in a healthy way. Moving to Colorado gave my family a chance to truly heal, then moving back to Maine with both sets of grandparents and the increased tensions between the families.

- Being okay with being misunderstood.
- Wanting that connection again with my husband.
- Rejection
- Questioning how I didn't know.
- Angry that a cold-hearted person could talk with me each time, show up at my baby shower, and even talk with me at church the week beforehand.
- Finding out that my brother-in-law and a close family friend had questioned Steve about having an affair back in October and never told me. All this came out in March 2017.
- Being high risk for postpartum depression—it was a miracle that did not happen to me. (If this is something that happens for you as a mother, it is okay and talk with your doctor sooner than later for your sake and the baby's sake.)
- Still wanting and choosing to celebrate the birth of our son.
- The hurt of close family members abandoning me again over our new son's birth. They were not in town for it on purpose because a business conference took priority. (If there was ever a time I needed them, it was at that point in any

capacity they could show up for it. Instead, they ran. Their priorities were way out of balance.)
- Loss of my niece and not seeing her grow up or having a relationship with her, even though I had watched her multiple days a week for more than a year.
- Seeing our older son be put through war. Dad gone, mom heartbroken, a new sibling, a big move, saying goodbye to grandparents who were visiting for the summer and then extended their stay when all this happened.

The top stressors in life are job loss, having a baby, moving, divorce, and death of a loved one, but yet he was still living. I had all of these at one time.

Practical Applications in My Story

If you find yourself in this situation, or one where trust is broken and sexual integrity is lost, then get yourself tested. Out of all the phone calls I had to make, calling my ob-gyn office was the hardest. I remember the nurse saying to me that they would have to test me for STDS, HIV, and other things, and depending on those results, talk about what type of birth would be best for me and the baby so as to not transfer anything to the baby during a vaginal delivery. I am very thankful to say that the baby and I had no ongoing effects from this part. That is a miracle, considering I knew that safeguards were not followed.

And through it all, I'm still standing. As Scripture says, when it gets tough, stand. And when you're not sure what else to do, stand. Some days it may be looking in the mirror and saying, "Well, I am still here, so here we go!" We have today, so we might as well make the most of it. Then, the moments, hours, and weeks when I was in shock and could not stand, those six friends stood for me. They held me up in prayer, in their presence, in the practical parts of life. When someone you know is going through a crisis, take the first step and show up for them however they would like you to. If they do not even know what they need, then do not expect them to tell you what you can do. *Take the first step by giving them the gift of your presence, and in that state the details will unfold.*

The image that keeps coming to my mind is Steve on the floor, a mess, and there I was pregnant and all, shielding him from all the naysayers and those who cast stones. Why? Would he have done it for me? Probably not. I did not do that for him. I am reminded of what Jesus did for me: unconditional love. How can I hold it against him? Forgiveness was more for me to let go of all the things that could destroy my heart than "making him pay." Is there justifiable anger? Yes. However, we cannot act out of anger or fear, but we do need to release it in healthy ways.

At the end of the day, I have to remember that it will be me before my heavenly Father. There will be no Steve next to me when I give an account of my actions on this earth. My children will not be there, nor will anyone else. Yet, I will give an account of what I allowed in my own life or what I knowingly allowed my children to be exposed to under the religious trauma of "just stick it out." *I say this firmly: if someone tells you something is off in their relationship at any point, believe them. Come alongside them and say, "What can I do to help?"*

I cannot picture Jesus responding with judgment, shame, condemnation, or walking the other way, and yet in so many religious circles, one would have thought I was the adulterer because of how it impacted their religious image. Two days after Steve walked out of our home, I got a call from our pastor's wife, and her phone call was with one thing in mind: to ask me not to say anything. She thought I was the one texting people and spreading the news. Are you kidding me? I was in shock, dealing with a husband who had completely imploded as a human, trying to get him the help he needed, and the purpose of her phone call was to protect the church image, not to mention a prominent member running for public office, and so a church scandal would not help the election. How about asking, "Are you okay, Sara?" How, as a church, can we support you? By the way, she had credentials in counseling and those were not being exercised on that phone call.

I ended up telling her I had nothing to do with that. I started to read all the names of unopened texts I got from their staff or members and said, "Looks like you need to teach your team how to lead in a crisis a bit more Christlike." She then asked me who was supposed to support me from the church, since the mistress' husband was on staff there, his folks were elders, and everything was connected.

I remember saying any elder's wife on staff could have offered support. Even the week before, there was a ladies church night, and the story they shared from the stage was now very similar to what I was living. I said to my pastor's wife, "That lady who shared her story at ladies' night and was also a respected leader in the church could have called me today instead of you, as she would have the proper motive." There was silence on the other side of the phone as that settled in. No apology, nothing for weeks to come from what was my own home church, and they too abandoned any support to me as someone who had been an active member, volunteer, event helper, and so on. Their focus was on image and not leadership. Out of the four adults involved in this situation, was it not a no-brainer that I needed the most help in this moment? Apparently, no. These are all things that are not okay or acceptable.

Jesus came to be with men and women on this earth. He did not come to create the litany of religions. Man created religion because they actually could not agree on their differences. How this must grieve Jesus' heart. I wonder what the world would look like if we actually operated as a unified church. *The church being if you profess to follow Jesus, you actually follow Jesus.* You show love to yourself and others. You give of your time, money, and resources, whether asked or not. You are so generous it does not even make sense to someone else because it is coming with no strings attached.

Jesus hung on that Cross and said, "Father, forgive them. They know not what they do." My sin is no better than someone else's. It doesn't mean there aren't consequences. It does mean it's all been forgiven when we confess it at the Cross. Each day I confess, "Lord, my life is not my own. Give me eyes to see my husband, my children, and those around me how You see them. Help my unbelief and let Your will be done in my life. Amen." The Sara today would also insert, "God, give me Your eyes to see me how You see me."

I was so focused on someone else's well-being that I had to remember to be kind to myself. Kindness may look like putting my phone down and going to sleep, even if it keeps going off from a partner who is out of line. I could not be sleep deprived with all that was on my shoulders in the immediate or ongoing turmoil. Kindness may look like eating properly for my own strength and the baby's strength, even when I have no appetite. Kindness meant that if I could not get back to everyone's phone calls, then it was what it was, because there was only so much bandwidth. I hope others can give grace and recognize that when a person is in crisis or ongoing turmoil, that is an unrealistic expectation, and frankly, that is more about you than how that helps them. What is helpful is prayer, gift cards, a note in the mail, sending flowers, or reaching out to someone close who is helping that person.

Practical Applications in My Story

During this immediate crisis time, I was surrounded by strong, close women friends of mine who literally delegated tasks, as I kept having to make decisions. One coordinated meals weekly for me, one provided childcare for our older son, one took me to doctor appointments, another sold items for money and our move, one helped me pack up our home, another was my emergency call for when it was time to go to the hospital to give birth, and so forth. I also want to thank their husbands because I know they held down my close women friends' homes in order to love and serve me and my broken family.

Then, as these ladies not only helped me on the logistical daily life side, they walked the emotional and heartbreak of it too with me. They gave me the courage to lean into the hard things, even in the shock of it all. I remember calling a close friend who was also a mentor of Steve and mine and how those families flew down to help mediate some real and immediate conversations. The amount of stress that comes in this type of situation is so high that you must call in someone who can be more objective for so many reasons. I would also say that during an immediate crisis, not everyone will show up how you hoped, and that is what it is. I am responsible for my actions and letting my needs be made known. I was doing as much as I could, but for anyone in the situation I was in, it is too much, and asking for help is important. *It is a choice of wisdom, not a sign of weakness.*

Change is hard for most people. This immediate crisis was the ultimate moment of change. The breach of trust in our marriage was a change; the pregnancy was a change; moving was a change; our family relationship and dynamics was a change; our older son's world completely changed, and being there for our older kids through these transitions is one thing, much less in a crisis. Finances changed. I remember going to the welfare office in California, and after that horrible experience for myself and our son, my friend was driving me and our son home, and I needed her to pull off to the side of the road because I needed to throw up. The waves of reality are change.

I remember having to go to the Colorado welfare office, and the experience was night and day. The ladies there were so kind. It was a clean office. They did not need to draw blood from me or my son. They treated me with dignity. One of the few things I did have left was my dignity. At these welfare offices, everything in my life was exposed even more and not from my own hands. It was nothing I ever wanted for myself or our kids.

It also is so very eye-opening to me. Why is my first place of ongoing financial support a government welfare office? Is my own home church, my close family, and friends that ungenerous? I grew up giving to the church my whole life. I grew up working hard and having a real job in high school, supporting myself all through college, and paying my way through school. I am not my husband's mistakes. And yet, I was left holding all the responsibility with literally no way to get a job, even if I wanted to. Who was going to hire a 35-week pregnant lady? How are we missing helping those in our own community? I think it requires all three: support the church, support organizations, and support those in your community. Maybe reach out and ask someone, how can we help? What do you need?

What is sad is that this situation affected the home church we went to; out of all four adults involved, I was the most needy and the last one to be contacted. I was, however, the first one to be called in order to keep it under wraps. The focus was on keeping their image intact and getting information out of me, rather than actually caring about me or my children as a whole. I often wonder what the world would look like if we were all actually generous with one another, with no strings attached.

In spite of more disappointments and compound hurts, I did not let that stop me. Once again, get informed. I made all kinds of phone calls to get practical advice (lawyers, mental health therapists, mentors) and in the end it was one moment and one decision at a time. Let the tears flow, blow your nose, and get back out there.

(Many years later, I have learned sadly that we do not value caregivers in our country or society. Hey, let's be on call 24/7 for eighteen years plus, and by the way, no paycheck, no health insurance, no benefits for retirement. Also, if something happens to you, the caregiver, well, no one knows who can then help take those responsibilities off your plate, whether you're well or not. And by the way, you're the one who knows your children best, wants to care for them with love and true protection, and if the partner you're supposed to be able to rely on screws you over, oh well, just go down to some random office that is not run like a business but treats you like a number and wait 1–2 years for help while your life is on fire. Oh, and when you're finally in a time of need, where is the church you've paid tithes to and served for weeks and years? Oh, and by the way, they give you random insurance, and you have to switch all your doctors but have to figure out which doctors in your area even take this insurance. Then, that's all going on while you're trying to just make a better life for yourself in the chaos.)

May I say once again, nothing is new under the sun, and it was actually the priest in biblical times that was the covering to the widows and children. Women were property back then, and the priest was the one that could vouch for her character. The priest was the one that would make sure her dowry was returned so she would not become destitute. The priest was the one that took care of her legal needs and new life. The priest was the one that made sure the widows and orphans were taken care of when the tithes and offerings came into the temple.

I think of the story of the woman at the well. One that has been preached so many times but without the historical elements discussed. When Jesus ends up saying to the woman that He knows she has had many husbands, that was so significant because only the priest in her town would have known that. He told her He is the water that she can drink from and never thirst again. *Jesus is revealing that He is her Great High Priest! I would submit that the answer in crisis is not to run to our government to financially, spiritually, emotionally, and physically take care of people, but the covering of our church with Jesus as the Great High Priest. Our leaders must be so educated and confident in navigating crisis that none "fall through the cracks," and destiny is not obliterated because the community surrounds each family.*

My family and children are not a number. We are people. We are human beings created in God's image. The mindset we need is that it is our privilege to make sure another human being created in the image of God is not cast aside. What if that was you? The irony is that it is each one of us. Our role is how will we respond.

The space of practical wisdom and being able to function or have a chance to heal. It is the space of the in-between.

From March 2017 until August 2017, we were in turmoil and the in-between. We both agreed to do a six-week intensive marriage therapy at a private practice. I found out the night before our last session when it was decision day that he still was lying through it all and still had not ended it with his new lover.

I took our now three-month-old and three-and-a-half-year-old to a friend's house for her to watch them while I went to our last couple's session, knowing that without a miracle, I had to say goodbye. It was not healthy or okay for this to keep continuing. From the first night back in March until the beginning of June, I had to put the marriage piece on hold because all the natural consequences that resulted from his decisions had to be addressed (i.e., where to live, income, bringing a baby into this world, the impact on our church world, family, and social connections; it was very public). I had to get on welfare to make it each month.

I may also write another book on empowering mothers to not have to choose between raising their baby and work. Taking care of your baby is harder and requires longer hours than work, and yet in our culture we expect mothers to do both or pick one and lose the other. (I want to explore how other countries value their women or caregivers as mothers or in other medical situations because life happens and is not linear.)

I remember getting to our session and sitting on the couch waiting for him to arrive. When I left our rental townhome, he was still sleeping on the couch at 9 a.m., and here I was up all through the night nursing, consoling our older son with night terrors, and trying to take care of myself as well. It was completely one-sided, but I had been operating like this way before now. It is so sad, but true.

The Unexplainable Miracle is Only God

I remember sitting on that couch in the therapist's office when Steve finally walks into the room. He sits down next to me like we had been doing, baseball hat pulled down almost covering his eyes, and so our therapist begins. I remember our therapist talking, but I was wrestling with my own conversation internally. I felt in my heart that I was supposed to reach over and grab his hand one last time. My head was like, "Heck no, Jesus, I am not touching him. Be grateful I have waited this long and that is enough." My spirit said just take his hand. I grabbed his hand with my left hand. I did not feel anything, but I remember seeing chills go up Steve's forearm, and he lifted his head to look at me. It was the first time he really was present and looked at me in months.

All confusion was gone, and the realization of his actions and that this opportunity to still choose his family was still before him filled him with joyful tears and true remorse, asking for forgiveness. Our therapist looked at me and I looked at him. Then, thank goodness, our therapist did the follow-up after that moment. Steve and I both agreed that we wanted to stay married and put in the hard work, but to do that, he had to end the affair. I had to set and keep boundaries or we had to be done as a couple.

Disclosure Note: Chapter 2–15 are thirteen chapters of my recovery process.

There are thirteen chapters of recovery. I ended up missing my own creative outlet while wading through this mess that I knew was a long road ahead of me, however it would look. I had a catering background and loved cooking and baking, but that was not happening with a newborn and toddler and a broken marriage, to say the least. I thought, "What about starting a soap company? It is similar to cooking, has a long shelf time and won't expire, and would also make the house smell good." I have never shared this part of my story, except with a close few, that each soap bar marked a significant step in my journey.

The following chapters are journal entries that marked the different stages in my own healing journey. Each entry is also a soap scent that marked that next new beginning, which was important to me because sometimes during hardships we may not be able to recognize that growth that is also happening simultaneously. I wrote these entries during these hard seasons of life and hope it can help bring the language to your own journey.

CHAPTER 2

Unscented

Coming Out of Crisis

I was in a place of not thinking I could dream again. Being in a crisis life can become unscented. It was a place of survival. Doing the basics each day was a goal enough in itself with all the responsibilities I had on my shoulders at that time.

Note: Some Days

Some days I just take a step back and look at the wake—the wake of a tsunami that crashed the shores of my heart. My family. My children.

I try to remember all the good times when it was once just us. Young and free to be just us. Then that's where I get hung up. Why can't it still be just us? Where along the line did you choose to leave me in the wake? When did you choose to leave our children in the wake and just choose yourself?

I look out over the devastation and find the pieces of our lives scattered on the shore, some to go out with the tide and to never return. I find torn photographs of our life as I hold my belly with new life inside. I think, "Can this be? Did this really just happen to me?"

Then the next tsunami hits, and this time it's my heart shattered in a million pieces, added to the rubble on the shores. I see it exposed. Betrayed. Rejected. Alone. I felt like I was being pummeled over and over again.

I hurriedly try to gather all the pieces as I choose to not let anything else be taken from me by the tide. I climb the sand dunes and stand on a rock. Gaze at that same ocean and am reminded of the Majesty of the God, whom I love and who loves me back more than I can ever imagine.

The sides of my being settle and peace floods those waters. My soul is restored and my feet firmly planted on the rock. I watch the sunset and darkness come. In that same spot, I watch the sun rise and a new day dawn. A new day for my miracle. A new day to be thankful for. And then, THE day comes. My miracle has come. I look out at the beaches again, and they are clear. The devastation is clear. The time has come for restoration, and new structures start to go up. It will take quite some time to see it finished. *Time is a conundrum. We wish it away sometimes, and then other times we hope to have it back. Be present in your present, for all days hold much to be desired, and some days seem just that, someday.*

The Road Less Taken— February 9, 2019

The road less taken. It's been buzzing around in my head, as I'm literally on the road less taken. It's a road many misunderstand, don't want to understand, and think I'm foolish for being on. And yet, I have all the peace there is. Peace to know I'm right where I'm supposed to be. Peace to let it go. All of it.

Whatever it is in your life, let it go and keep on walking down the road less traveled. Few find this road, but when you do, it is a road that in the end leads to the Savior's loving arms. It is the best place to be on this side of eternity and into the next. Which road is less taken in your life? Are you on it?

Jesus Bears All the Pain— February 2019

You used to make my face hurt from all the smiling, and now it hurts from tears of pain. The pain of a broken heart. The pain of betrayal, of dreams undone. It didn't have to be this way. You chose yourself and left the rest of us in the wake of pain. Pain that our Savior bore on the Cross. I used to think that Jesus bearing our pains and sorrows meant our physical pain and tough times. Now, it takes on a whole new meaning for me. Who can bear the pain of a broken heart but Jesus? For He heals the brokenhearted and sets the captives free.

My present day is that of a broken heart and my need to be set free from the horrible mind cycles of the past wrongs, so I don't miss the present-day rights. The rights of it being us now. Our children now. Our family intact. The rights of a job, home, emotional healing through counseling, and great family and friends. The rights of having good health and food on our table. The rights of being able to be the one to raise my baby and older son and not have those firsts or beginning years given to another. Even in the pain, fight for your soul, your family. Remember the rights in your life and let go of the wrongs. Hold fast to your Savior, Jesus. For He loves you with an unconditional love that no man will ever match or compare.

Broken heart, take your time to heal. Give yourself the grace to cry, the freedom to laugh again, and let love endure.

Good Friday—March 2019

Good Friday is a day we stop to remember the greatest act of love our heavenly Father made. Putting His Son on the Cross for my sins, our sins. At the same time, how frustrating, how easy, intentional, divine, unconditional, giving, patient He is with us!

Through the mess that Steve and I went through, I stopped and reflected and realized that God the Father gave me a unique and rare opportunity to be in His shoes, to choose to lay down my life for another each day as Steve rejected my love, our covenant with Christ, and Jesus' free gift of forgiveness. Scripture says how He stands at the door and knocks, and all we have to do is let Him in. People ask me and say, I can't believe you were able to forgive him—to treat him with respect and such grace. Honestly, as angry as I was and still am at times, it was that anger of love. Scripture says God is a jealous God, and that vengeance is His. Well, that's because we are made in His image and are His creation. Just as I knew Steve was mine through our covenant of marriage, until he was willing to choose Christ and to choose to accept His forgiveness, it was out of my hands but to be present. Present with my love; present with my actions to point Steve towards Christ. And truly, the love of Christ is what brings us to repentance.

It was easy to forgive Steve because I had been forgiven by Christ. It was extremely hard and hurtful to be rejected continually, lied to, and questioned. But yet, isn't that what Jesus went through with those who have not yet discovered their faith in Christ or even heard about what Jesus did for them, being the ultimate sacrifice so that we didn't have to? Wow, I'm so grateful to have a small glimpse into what the Father felt when He sent His Son.

    Why did Jesus stay the course? Why did I not give up on Steve? Because Steve was my beloved and I was his, even when he couldn't or didn't want to see it. Then, that's when faith and the love of Christ breaks down every wall, every chain, every point of darkness. I called him out of the darkness and into the light each day. And each time, the darkness cannot stay in the light of God's love. There was nothing I could do, manipulate, or whatever else. Because it's a free gift for anyone to believe, and they have to accept it because they want to. I couldn't make Steve stay with me. And I didn't want to. I wanted him to stay because he wanted to stay. You can never run from grace. Steve tried, and even if he didn't choose me and his family, he still could not run from the love of God.

    In our marriage that last week, when it was all put on the line, that Tuesday I did end it and say I was done after Steve told me he was divorcing me and then reneged. That was the final boundary for me. You don't tell your wife that it is for real this time with a close male friend there as a mediator, and then the next day in an emergency session, say you didn't mean that.

    I'll never forget that day, but I also will never forget three days later in our final session—when I felt the Holy Spirit tell me to reach over and touch Steve's hand—how I saw chills go up Steve's arm, and he said everything became so clear. The confusion was gone. He could see all his choices for what they truly were. Steve didn't know it, but after Tuesday I emailed our therapist and told him I was open to reconciling if come

Friday he's all in and truly will end it with her. That was a miraculous moment where a marriage that had been declared dead had a Lazarus moment and was resurrected by the power of Jesus Christ three days later. And now, a year later, I can sit here today and say yes, Lord, and amen. We're still standing!

Some of the most painful times in our lives are also the greatest opportunities to see God move in our lives. At times, this process seemed to focus all on Steve, but that was not entirely the case, as each day I still struggle and work through the internal dialogue of what God says about me and not what Satan is telling me through fear, doubt, worry, and resentment. Just remember, everything bows at Jesus' name! Praise God!

CHAPTER 3
Relaxing Lavender

Relieving Stress—May 2018

I needed something to give my mind a rest. When you go through longer periods of crisis, you have to find your anchors of relief or you will not make it well. Ironically, I needed something outside of anything family-related or for someone else. I needed an outlet for me. That was when I experimented with soap making, and later down the road it turned into a business. A business to help people remember to take time and moments to sit down to have face-to-face conversations with people, kids, or your significant other. Just be present. Soap making for me was me being present for Sara. That was the greatest gift I could give myself and my family. I cannot take care of anyone else well if I am not taking care of myself first. Plus, we needed the money; it helped the house smell good, and it also was a great mental, emotional, and physical outlet for me.

(Later in that journey of soap making, I had a studio in our basement. It was nothing huge, but it met my needs. It was where I could dream and laugh with close friends on the phone as I made the soap bars, cry, pray, and just be, Sara.)

CHAPTER 4
Wild Vanilla

Staying the Course and Showing Up—May 2018

Raising littles may seem vanilla, but it is anything but. It was a wild time: moving, nursing, bottles, pumping, diaper changing, night terrors for our older son. This soap scent also smells like cookies, and ironically, this was the first time in my life I finally figured out how to make baller chocolate chip cookies.

Email I Sent My Close Friend in 2019

Even in our own sorrows we learn to encourage ourselves and do not forget to encourage others too.

For some momma out there.

You're right where you're supposed to be. Stay the course, raise those kiddos, love yourself despite how your body may have once looked. It's not going to be this way forever. It's just today. That's it. Keep your eyes on the present. Your body just carried, loved, grew, and birthed this baby into the world. Whether you're nursing or doing bottles, you're enough! You haven't failed. You have loved and love wholeheartedly. Let the tears out, blow your nose and try again. Your kids need you; your family needs you; this world needs you!

Motherhood is one of the most beautiful gifts in life, the most refining process of dying to self, and the most rewarding to be entrusted with a life. One that we, as mothers, learn to nurture, try, fail, and get back up again. We teach them to hear the voice of the Holy Spirit for themselves, so when we aren't there, they know they are never alone. Christ is with them. Then we learn to let them go, for their next season has just begun, whether it is kindergarten, getting their license, going into the military, college, starting a new business, and so forth. We love them, pray for them, cry with them, and laugh with them.

So mother, don't be so hard on yourself. You're one amazing lady inside and out. When you miss it, admit it, forgive yourself, and love the person God's called you to be.

Caretakers can only be there if they are taking care of themselves first. You're not alone. I love you; God loves you; and I'm sure your momma loves you too.

The Love of a Mother— February 2019

Who can comprehend the love of a mother until you've become a mother yourself? I'm thankful for the gift of bearing children, nursing, and raising my children. It all goes by so fast, yet in the moment it can feel so long. I caution mothers who are in the struggles of postpartum stages, young children's stages, to remember the gift you have before you, accept the help you need in moments, and give yourself the grace to let things go.

Let go of the image of a "perfect" family. No one's family is perfect, nor will we ever be. Just be together. Sort through house responsibilities. Include your husband, extended family, or even a cleaning service so you don't burn yourself out. Your husband and your children just want you, and the rest takes a backseat. Rest when you can rest!

Hold on to your dignity, your forgiveness, your candor. Hold on to those late nights and early morning moments. Be present and put the phone away.

Embrace the mom bun, hair dye, multiple-sized clothes through different stages. That's what our bodies are supposed to do!

What better time in life to explore curves, large boobs, small boobs, athletic calves, or skinnier legs.? We were made to give life physically, mentally, and emotionally to others and to get the help we need for ourselves. It was through a woman's womb that a Savior came for the whole world! What!

And for those whose wombs have lost life, who have not been yet opened to bear life, I pray God's peace rests in your soul, your spirit, and your body. I pray you do not lose hope and remain steadfast in your present day. I pray the Giver of all things gives you a new life and opens what has been closed. I pray for comfort and healing to those wounds and memories.

At what point will our culture applaud the mother? I don't think it will, but I will! You moms out there—great job! You have done more, seen more, sacrificed more than any other "professional" out there. You are the most revered professional there is.

I've made two humans, potty trained, trained, cooked 1,095 meals a year for at least four people each night, made 2,190 snacks a year, balanced our budget for the last eight years, flipped a house and made a profit while being pregnant and having a newborn, got a bachelor and graduate degree, moved seven times, flown hundreds of flights, managed multiple family relationships. So yes, I think I can deal with you and whatever may arise in this "office" as opposed to my "home" office. So what was your question about the gap in my resume?

The perspective towards mothers just bugs me. It's the greatest privilege and job out there. And do you know the mothers that are even more qualified? Single moms! They are some of the toughest, most go-getter women who should not be looked down upon but have so much to offer. It's because of a mother's love that drives us because it's not about us, ourselves, anymore. We need more love shown in this world. We need the love of a mother.

CHAPTER 5

Pine Scrub

Going Back to the Basics— May 2018

This soap scent was Steve's request. It's practical for outdoor spaces and keeps bugs away. We were supposed to do porch chats even once a week for ten minutes, but we still haven't gotten that figured out yet. I'm not proud of that fact, but it is ever so important to take uninterrupted time with your spouse in the small moments without it needing to be some big planned event monthly. Build character in the mundane, and the fancier times are icing on the cake.

   This was a time for being that much more intentional with everything we were working on in therapy individually and as a couple. I would suggest any time this type of breach of trust happens in a marriage, you need all three of those elements: individual therapy for both persons and couples therapy for the two of you together. The unhealthy part of our relationship in the healing stages was Steve weaponizing what we would learn in therapy for manipulation. This is extremely unhealthy. I say that because if someone else finally makes it to this part in their own relationship, I want them to realize it will take an unknown amount of time to heal as individuals or as a couple.

Each person has their own process, and each person has their own free will. I had to learn to recognize these unhealthy patterns and accept the person (myself and Steve) who is standing in front of me and not the person I hope them to be.

CHAPTER 6
Orange Citrus

Right Relationships— March 2018

Steph and I made this soap together. I'm thankful to have my sister and our relationship back on the right path after many years.

My sister, Steph…where to start? I would say I have always loved her dearly, and for many years in our early adult years, our relationship was strained. The year during the affair, she and my mom did stop by our home in California before their trip, and those were big steps in a new direction. It was not anything super long, but steps we both took toward one another, then away from one another. Later, after all this came out, it was also my sister (who I had not seen in person for far too long) that picked up on something being off in my own home, even when I did not. I would say take what others have to say, process it for yourself, and then go from there. I would also say, if there are strained relationships between you and a sibling, continue to reach out in what is appropriate because you never know what they may be facing and vice versa, and you need to be present for one another. This soap scent marked for me a sweet season where we both had consistently been back in each other's lives for years now.

Little did I realize that only a few short years later, she would have not only one stroke but two. I'm thankful we made the most of our relationship then and still are to this present day. In this situation, you are grieving the very person you love right in front of you as you take care of them. On the flip side, that loved one is grieving all of their losses in real time in front of the people they love. They are fully aware and yet cannot even touch, talk, or move towards their loved ones.

My sister had a stroke that took out half of her body, left her with double vision and no speech, and then it happened again two years later. I was grieving the sister I once had in every way. I was grieving her grief of loss and speaking words of life and hope over her. Her very living presence each day is a true reminder of the miracle of her life. Steph's body is just that—her own body—but Steph is truly the spirit living in her body, reminding her of what matters most. I will never regret not taking a family member or friend's phone call. The more I walk with Jesus, the more evident it becomes to be simple. Simplify in every way.

The most valuable commodity is not money, but time. Once it is gone then it is gone.

CHAPTER 7
Cedarwood Spice

Forgiveness—September 2018

My older son and I made this soap together. This felt like the first time I could really just enjoy being his mom again and not have to filter through all of life's other demands. One of the hardest things for me is forgiving Steve for taking away the joy of being a stay-at-home mom to our children. For easily four solid years, crisis stole all that time and energy I wanted to pour into my children. That was my desire and what our family core value was—for me to be able to stay home in their younger years.

Stories—February 2019

I can't help but think about the fact that my husband is such an amazing and gifted storyteller. He captures people's lives and moments and is able to clearly communicate them to the masses, sometimes with words and sometimes without.

Then I think of our story. Is it one we will hold close just for the few? Or is it one that at some point we will share with the masses? Either way, I am not sure. I just know I am yours, Jesus, and wherever, whomever you want me to cross paths with, is quite all right with me. How freeing is that?! To just rest in the Father's arms.

My marriage is far from repaired. The path of recovery is one that takes perseverance, consistency, honesty, and humility. It's one that only I can do with the saving knowledge and power of Jesus Christ.

CHAPTER 8
Sweet Honeysuckle

Grieving: Death of a Dream—April 2019

Betsy passed away, which was a literal death and death of a dream.

Betsy was like a second mom to me. She used to watch me and my sister when we were growing up and my mom was a single mom. Her sudden passing from a heart attack rocked my world, as I used to call her late at night sitting in the Wal-Mart parking lot to get diapers or formula for the week. My milk had dried up at four months from all the stress. We were on government programs to help cover our needs, too. Her wisdom and continual encouragement kept me going. She never made me feel embarrassed by my marriage situation, and I so wish she could have met our new baby boy. Her memorial service was the same weekend our baby was born, only two years later. Because of her passing, this was also the first time I flew back to Maine since the break in our marriage. (Both Steve and I were from the same hometown, as we had known each other since high school and met in youth group.)

Ironically, I am thankful I went by myself and faced a host of memories of what once was. There were memories of Steve and our love story all over that city. Where we met, got engaged, our childhood homes, high schools, churches, the church we got married in, seeing my parents together, and so forth. It was Betsy's literal death—the death of a dream that she could meet and see my little family. And with that time of the year being our youngest son's birthday, it was the death of how his birth and our present life were supposed to be. It was time to grieve the loss and then time to move through the loss.

I Miss Us—February 2019

I miss so many things that once were. I'm not looking to wallow in the past. I am looking to work through the sting of betrayal.

I miss the trust we had in each other. I never thought you'd want to share your heart with another. I still don't understand the *why* behind it all. What love story could you possibly have that you believed was true? It couldn't have been the part where you're married and she's married to one of the pastors at the church we attend. You're married with a son and have another baby on the way. Or the part that she's the pastor's wife of the church we attended as a family together and a coworker at our school alma mater? That's where our love story happened. That's where we celebrated with friends our engagement in purity and joy.

The part that hurts the most is that you had no thought of anyone else—me, your wife, your children, our whole world together. The most unnerving part of it all is how good you were at living a double life without a trace. I saw you losing patience or spiritually not wanting to do things as a family or together or by yourself. I gave you the benefit of the doubt. He's stressed at work, and there are more transitions with moving and with the baby.

In my opinion, there is no excuse for bad behavior, and I would not lose the man I know you are, or more so, who God's called you to be. I made every effort for two years before this to get you, me, and us the help we needed. And yet something did happen. Something I never dreamed was possible. How could this have happened? Am I a fool to have given you the benefit of the doubt? Thinking he's okay; he's telling me he's okay. I never ever imagined the magnitude of what was happening. And at the end of the day, I was completely blindsided and left with nothing but my son and unborn child. Two of the most beautiful gifts from God, and yet my heart utterly shattered, my soul weeping, and my spirit keeping me steady.

My mind went in a thousand directions over those immediate minutes, hours, days, and months following. I was 35 weeks pregnant, and you came to every appointment. (Why? I don't get it. You didn't care about me when you loved another that was not yours to love.)

In the biggest betrayal of my life, the man who was supposed to protect me and his children, spiritually lead our family together, provide, and show our children God's love through his earthly example, tossed us like a piece of trash and continued to for months to come, even after telling me about the affair and then leaving with no communication but a note left on the counter that says "I'm sorry."

I'm sorry—two words that still haunt me to this day. At that moment, I had no idea what all those two words were supposed to be apologizing for besides knowing he'd had an affair. I knew it happened a few times, but that was all he could get out.

Those two words, "I'm sorry," couldn't even cover the new reality my world and my children's world were thrown into. And even if Steve didn't realize it or think it through, I recognized he needed me now more than ever, even though I'm the person he's running from. I knew in my spirit that I had to step up and protect him, love him, get him the help he needed.

In the hours, days, and weeks unfolding, I lost my spouse, my children lost their father, Steve lost his job, and we had no income. We had almost two and a half months in savings, which would cover costs up to me being pregnant and post-recovery. I lost my home. The money was in the house since we renovated it, and I couldn't stay knowing what had occurred in my own home. I couldn't get a job because I was about to have a baby, and who would hire an almost full-term pregnant lady? I lost my home church support, as they were more concerned about the image of the church and those two than realizing that out of the four adults involved, I was the one most in need.

When it was all stripped away and I looked myself in the mirror, the Holy Spirit ever so sweetly reminded me that I am yours and you are mine. I looked at my wedding ring in disgust, and again, I am yours and you are mine. My grace is sufficient for you. All these scriptures I had stored in my heart came pouring out. And an overwhelming peace flooded my soul. Jesus, my life has always been Yours. Give me Your eyes to see. And Jesus did, each step of the way.

I question constantly how we got to this place in our marriage when I tried over and over with Steve, and he'd participate in the counseling but not put forth the effort to work on it consistently. It took this kind of heartbreak for him to finally put forth the effort because "now" I'm worth it. We're worth it. I was the best thing that's happened to him, and vice versa, when we got married. How does a person throw that all away? I wonder, will I ever get over it? Can I get to the day where I can fully relax and give my heart completely to him or him give his heart completely to me? I know we each gave the other our heart when we renewed our vows, so why is that a constant unsettling in me? I know that my trust has to be rebuilt.

It's weird that I even have to question that. My dream and covenant I made with him seven years ago was to forsake all others. And he didn't. But we came into our marriage in purity. We followed after Christ wholeheartedly. How, as a spouse, do you cope with infidelity? Abandonment? Rejection? Selfishness? Anger? Much less have a baby, sell a home, move across the country, and then face your new normal of facing Steve and figuring out this mess. I was functioning as a single mother, and yet I was still married. That's not how it's supposed to be…

I truly believe I tried to the best of my ability to show Steve Christ's love. I know I wasn't perfect, nor was that my standard. When I let my flesh get the best of me, I'd apologize and own up to it. I have come to realize that Christ's love is unconditional. And as much as it pains me personally, the choices he made were his choices, not mine. I am responsible for my actions, and first it's showing Steve the Father's love. Above all else, whether he stayed or left, I knew he needed to find himself in Christ. It was his journey, not mine. But as long as I was in his life, then I hoped and prayed God would move in Steve's life, as well as mine and our children's.

I still choose Christ. I still choose my spouse. I still choose forgiveness. I still choose new beginnings.

I may grieve the loss of many things, but I'm praying this will pass, as I'm tired of crying over what cannot change. I just don't want to be naïve, which I don't think I am, but this whole situation makes me question so much. I want to continue to build a foundation for us now. And thank You, Jesus, for this second chance to do just that.

CHAPTER 9

Peppermint Eucalyptus

New Beginnings— April 2019

This scent evokes new beginnings and healing. At some point, you have to forgive, put the past behind you, and live in the present.

The more I have been on this journey of reconciliation, the more I realize new beginnings can be so beautiful and painful at the same time. See the beauty, acknowledge the pain, and embrace the present. I finally got to a place personally and with professional ongoing therapy to realize I am going to embrace the present, even when it is not how I think it should be. Starting new friendships, working through imposter syndrome of people thinking "they are all good now," and really still riding the waves of a very reactive and emotional spouse, on top of taking care of my own needs, my children's needs, our home, and my business.

I would encourage you to show up. Show up just as you are. If people judge you, want to ask probing questions, and are not in your inner circle, then do not feel like you have to prove anything. Be kind in your answer, and it can be as easy as "we're working through some things." That is it. I learned once you have dealt with some very hard traumas, it is not my responsibility to catch others up on the process, nor for me to go back to wherever they left off. You are in a new beginning, and so embrace it!

CHAPTER 10

Pumpkin Spice

Letting Creativity Flow— August 2019

This is the second soap I made with our older son. Our family has always loved the fall, and this was a great way to kick off a big transition for our older son by going into kindergarten.

This was also another time of transition for him going to school and Steve and I agreeing on what that looked like for our family. Ironically, he only went to public school for a semester and a few months, as then the pandemic hit in March 2020, and we did the last of his kindergarten year that spring virtually with his public school. We got creative with the soap making, with his schooling, and then I went back to finish my five master classes fully online that spring as well in 2020.

CHAPTER 11

Espresso Delight

Gaining Confidence Again—October 2019

This was a collaboration with a coffee roaster in town. This soap scent was so fun for me to make as I got to experiment and try new things. Two years later, I was in a better place, and this felt like life was somewhat normal again. This soap gave me my confidence back. I knew I enjoyed motherhood, but this reminded me I still had it in the business world as well.

This was also the time when I decided to look into how to finish graduate school. I looked to transfer to other universities in the Midwest, but because I was so far into the program I was in, it did not make sense to transfer, as I was going to lose so much time and money. Then, I looked into seeing how I could finish at our alma mater. This was a place where so many dreams had been made for me. I was the first in my family to go to college and finish, much less do a master's program. I picked up with Steve and our relationship again when I transferred to California from Texas. I worked on campus as a student and then came back to live on campus with Steve and our oldest son as a staff family. I got to bring our son to see where his parents' love story transitioned into marriage. Then, this is also where it poetically fell apart too.

I faced all those fears, and I learned that I had missed the two-year hold withdrawal period by a few months and needed to reapply to the program. Thankfully, I got accepted back into the program and finished the five classes by putting some soap money aside to pay for school and for books. In each class, I truly enjoyed learning. From a very young age, I have always loved learning new things and discovering how they work. This season was one where week by week I gained my confidence back, even with whatever was going on around me.

I would also say that prior to getting accepted back into graduate school, my focus could finally shift more back to me. The focus on Steve and the kid's needs was still happening, but I had to learn to still operate and not give up my own needs.

Letter to Myself — Remember March 26, 2020

Sara,

Even if Steve is not for you, I am for you. (God is for you.) Remember this. In every season, He made a way. He provided spiritually, mentally, and emotionally. He provided for you, for your kids, for Steve. Even when Steve could not see His mercies, He was ever so gracious.

When God is for you, who can be against you? Who in this world or the one we cannot see be against you? Those attacks fall at the name of Jesus. No sickness or disease, plague, or fear can stand in the holiness of Jesus. Doing this life map reminds me of His favor, faithfulness, provision, divine intervention.

He saved my life from death (a truck almost ran me over as a child; tried to take my life), car accident (tried to take my finances), affair (tried to take my family). BUT JESUS! When Jesus rose from the dead, that was the final moment where even death no longer had the final say.

Remember to teach your sons to forgive, trust God, give, and share God's love.

Remember to rest in the peace and provision of almighty God.

Remember to pray like you never have before.

Remember to not lose the Hope we have in Jesus.

Love you, Sara. You and Jesus got this,

S

I was learning mostly how to encourage myself. To not be in survival mode any longer, but to just be. Three years later, and all the changes I could never imagine, good or bad, we have today. Show up for the day.

CHAPTER 12
Soothing Sandalwood

New Normal and COVID—April 2010

The pandemic hit, and what better way to enjoy the house than needing something calming? Sandalwood was chosen, as this was around the time our close friends got matched for their international adoption, and sandalwood is from India. I wanted to make this soap to remember their first match, who passed away, and also to pray for their current daughter, who they were now going to adopt.

Learn to find your calm in the storm. For me, it was my faith. I would say I am a spiritual person who is a Christ-follower. The Jesus I follow is one who is in my present. Not pushy, He is there when He is invited to be. He offers the greatest gift of free will. The Jesus that sits with people right where they are. The Jesus that knows our needs even before we do and meets them. *The Jesus that values women in their God-given role on this earth. He did not limit women's abilities but gave them the greatest responsibility of nurturing life.* I love the analogy of a woman being the art and the man being the frame. One is not more important than the other. They both have their roles and purpose, and yet both complement one another. I wonder what our world would be like if we truly valued both roles. Would it bring calm to the chaos?

CHAPTER 13
The City Blend

Thankfulness— September 2020

I could not have been more thankful than to come back to Colorado. This city truly has been the place for me and my family to heal. I was not sure how it would all look, and that was okay. I knew that if there was any place we could heal, then this was that place.

Colorado. Every place we have lived, each location holds a sweet part of my heart, whether in good times or bad times. Colorado may not have made sense to many in the moment, but I had that peace. Relationship-wise, we had support there; it was where our therapists could help us, and it was the last chapter in our marriage when it was good before moving back to California. It was also known logistically for me with a newborn since I had our older son here in Colorado. Financially, it was far more affordable and neutral ground. Colorado has the most awesome breastfeeding clinic available for mothers at any stage of their feeding journey for their babies and littles.

This city was also where we launched Steve's business, which helped us get back on our feet financially, as we used the last of our savings to launch the company. It was also the season where we moved into our first home post everything. This was where we raised our kids. I did first grade with our oldest by day during the pandemic, graduate school by night, my soap business in the gaps of the day with naptimes, and saw myself for who I was once again. I am still Sara with my faith in Jesus. Loving myself, letting others help and speak into my life and our marriage too. Letting my needs be made known and riding those waves of change as I was the one that enabled too many unhealthy patterns as well when it came to "holding the home down." That pendulum needed to swing to a healthier place post the immediate and ongoing crisis period. This part in a recovery journey can feel like you're ripping off yet another Band-Aid, but let it rip. *Enabling someone else's poor behavior is actually the most unloving thing you can do to them.*

CHAPTER 14

Crisp Evergreen

Making New Memories— November 2020

Christmas, for me, has been a hard season in my life. This was not always the case, but when the rug is pulled out from under you and you do not even realize those were your last moments as a family, it just hurts. For me, Christmas 2016 was the last holiday that Steve was even somewhat nice to me, despite everything going on in his life that was deceptive. It is partly why, as a small business owner, I have had a hard time wanting to even think about Christmas, as it hits those triggers in me with suspicion. Is this my last time as a family again? This year I have chosen that hope is dangerous, as it does leave you open to being hurt again. However, I would rather hope than build walls that leave me isolated and everyone else out. Choose hope, my friends.

Note: December 2020

I heard it said once, "If the disease or crisis doesn't destroy you, your own mental health can, if you let it."

I know I have talked quite a bit about being present. Part of that is being intentional with making new memories, whether it is planned or organically happens. Even when I did not have the money for vacations or even eating out, I would be intentional with myself or my children in making memories. For myself, it may look like taking ten minutes each day outside, getting some sun. Close friends would know if I have been taking time for myself if my natural tan was on point in the summer. It was free; I was getting vitamin D; I would listen to the birds or the wind around me; it grounded me to transition for the second half of the day before hitting the third shift through the night. Once again, finding an anchor may not mean starting a business. It can be as simple as five to ten minutes for just you.

For my children, it may look like working with whatever you have. We would make airplanes and draw pictures on paper grocery bags. We turned the garage in our townhome into a playroom by putting cheap carpet scraps down, and kids would even stop in to play after school. When we moved into our home, the water was from a well and was my lifesaver through Covid. I would have our youngest do all different types of water play while teaching our older son science out back in the yard for the afternoon part of the day, then the boys would just be kids. Even in the winter months, I would fill up the bathtub and do all kinds of fun water games. Things that could sink or float, or beads (I do not recommend that in a bathtub but outside if they are biodegradable), bubbles, bath bombs, stacking plastic cups, swimming, and more. Parents may want to rush through bath time, but that can also be your greatest ally. It let off the last bit of energy from the day, gave me a few minutes to be in the bathroom and wrap up the last texts or emails I needed to do, and kept everyone's hygiene on point, and then off to bed.

CHAPTER 15
Closing Chapter

What I Learned

Hope is real, and hope makes you vulnerable. Hope can also take you to places of healing as well. Hope can mean and look different for each person. For me, my hope was to give my marriage and family a true chance at reconciliation. For that, I am thankful, as we have had that chance. Presently, my hope is for continued growth in healthy boundaries in my marriage and in how that needs to look between Steve and me.

I still don't think Steve realizes how much he hurt me. And I'm not sure if he can handle hearing it or should even hear it at this point. However, this is my journey and story. For the first few years, I focused way too much on him, and now, in this part of my life, that pendulum is swinging back to a healthier version of me where it needs to be.

I had to learn to forgive and let the resentment go. I had to learn to feel the anger and process through it. One time, this looked like being a part of Fit Body Bootcamp. My gracious best friend came with me to a few of those sessions, even in the early hours of the morning. I remember part of the circuit was medicine ball throwing and rope burpees. At the end of that exercise circuit, the instructor came over and said, "Looks like that was a good one for you." I realized throwing the medicine ball down for reps was a great outlet for releasing anger that I needed to let out in a healthy way before going home to pump for bottles, nurse, or do formula bottles, too.

I learned that I was too dependent financially. Religious trauma and manipulation played a huge unhealthy role as to how I thought a marriage should operate, and yet my needs were constantly pushed to the side. We place far too much responsibility on young men getting married in their early twenties to lead their families. They are not grown up enough to even lead themselves, much less take on another person, children, finances, and so forth.

I want to dispel some of the speculation and comments that were posed to me so callously so that when you are faced with this same type of deception, you can realize what you are dealing with spiritually as well. I also want to give the disclaimer that some people are not aware of these types of complex layers (not trauma informed, personality disordered informed, spiritually informed, or have ever dealt with someone that has high traits of narcissism can understand without living it). Also, a key indicator of these elements is the person causing these dysfunctions still presenting themselves as a victim rather than taking accountability for their own decisions.

Things that were said to me by other people accusing me of why my husband made the decisions he made and somehow thinking that could rationalize and justify his actions. *There is nothing on my end that justifies my spouse to commit adultery, continue to weave cobwebs of lies, to keep ongoing sin hidden, and all the rest.* I hope my being vulnerable in sharing these below will help you reframe and understand the truth and let you know to trust yourself!

PHRASE 1

"Well, Sara, you were pregnant and must have had a hard pregnancy and not giving him sex and that is why he had to cheat."

TRUTH OF PHRASE 1

We still were having sex 4–5 times a week, and I had a wonderful pregnancy health wise (or so I thought). Thankfully, I am the type of woman who loves being pregnant and never dealt with morning sickness or any other complications each time. Also, he was not using protection, and the week after the truth came out, I had to get tested for all sorts of STDs to see if I could even deliver vaginally with my unborn child so as not to pass any sexually transmitted diseases to my child. No one wants to talk about that because it is the hard truth, and I was having sex with my husband without fully knowing what I was consenting to with him. Why would I have thought there was a risk? It was just me and him, right, especially with both coming into our marriage as virgins, too. Wrong!

PHRASE 2

"He had a lot on his plate, and you were not there for him emotionally. That is why he found comfort with his coworker."

TRUTH OF PHRASE 2

If anything, I had more on my plate with raising a family, getting my master's degree, facilitating a house renovation, and meeting all his needs as well. Recovering people pleaser over here, by the way! What he was responsible for was going to work each day, which he did. Then he wanted his cake and ate it too, as there was a porn addiction I had no idea about, and this was him using his coworker to fulfill all those different fantasies. Also, he was manipulating me to fulfill those sexual fantasies at home, too, and with me being pregnant. Who is that all about? Him and his gratification at any cost.

PHRASE 3

"How could you not know?"

TRUTH OF PHRASE 3

I am sorry that I believe the best in others and am not a controlling person. I do not think like a person with sexual addictions because I am not a sex addict. All I saw different at home was that our communication took a hit. The further he went into the affair and sexual immorality, the worse he spoke to me and our children at home. I also did not continue to enable that behavior and got us into couples therapy, as we needed help.

In one moment, I lost my spouse and my home. He lost his job, and rightfully so. I was about to have a baby, and I needed to then do a cross-country move, too. He was a master at leading a double life, with no repentance at all. Full adultery, abandonment, and no repentance looked me in the face one evening as I folded laundry on our master bedroom bed. (I came to find out later they had sex in our home in that bed as well.) He said he was leaving and ran out of the house crying and a full coward.

Oh, but somehow, he is the victim according to all his enablers and "flying monkeys." *Remember, healing and freedom can only come when it is brought to the light.* Then, when it is brought to the light, may those people that receive the hard news not shove those causing these heartbreaks back into the darkness by not allowing them to take accountability for their actions.

Do not take their dignity once their deeds come to the light. *Failure is the best teacher if we love people enough to let them learn from it.* If we love them enough to feel and walk out their own consequences, then the chances of it being repeated are far less.

In our family's situation, I enabled too many parachutes, extended family enabled too many parachutes, as did the church community. What I thought was a rebuilt foundation ended up being anything but that.

On the practical and cultural side of being in the United States, I learned we do not value the caregiver as a mother. In this situation, there was no way for me to stand on my own two feet and still stay at home full time with our children. We are in 2022, and still women have to choose between family and money. Me choosing to stay home with our children is my full-time job and does not have set hours, sick days, paid vacation, 401k matching funds, or anything else. Staying home is the harder decision.

Why is there not a way to stay at home with your young children and still know that the job you had before transitioning into motherhood was working for you? The company values you as an employee so much that there is paid paternity and maternity leave because family is what matters most for whatever profession and not because I had to save all my sick days for over five years before having children. Once again, more hoops soon-to-be mothers have to jump through, and yet our culture loves when women give birth because that alone is a BILLION-dollar business, but we do not love nor provide great post-delivery care or ongoing benefits for mother and child. Instead, the message is given that it is good to be a working full-time woman while pregnant, but once that main event of giving birth happens, we choose to vaporize that woman. Where does she end up going but back to the same crossroads of family or money?

In my situation, it would cost me more money than what I was able to make by going back to work full time. In the end, I would miss raising my newborn and three-and-a-half-year-old, and I would have to pay someone else to do that. I would work long hours and days and multiple jobs to make ends meet. Yet, I could not work too much and go over said amount of money or else I would lose the one welfare benefit I was eligible for, which was some extra support for groceries that covered milk, eggs, certain types of formula (and hope that my baby can tolerate those types), and bread. Not to mention, still carrying the stress of sorting out a broken marriage and taking time, even for my own needs. Then we wonder as a society why families deteriorate so quickly? I would argue a big factor in that is because we do not make it a priority to help keep them together, especially during the most vulnerable years of babies and young children. We truly do not support women in whatever path of motherhood she would like to take.

I will go even further to ask the question, "In our culture, do we truly value caregivers?" The answer is no based on the research, and yet everyone truly values the caregiver when they are fully dependent on that person or persons. Then, they are desperately looking for the best situation for care for their own needs. It is sad but true; in our culture, we value self. What makes me happy? What do I get out of it? How can it help me?

I wanted to be self-sufficient, and there was no way I could do both in the position I found myself navigating. Why is there such a disconnect in our country? The greatest gift we can give to ourselves and our families is us. What happens when the family unity falls apart? In my story, there were no options for me to stay in my own home even if I wanted to. The only other option was to borrow money from family and then pay them back once the house sold. Even then, not everyone has family that could or would be willing to lend the money or can sell a home for a profit. Even for mothers that are more than financially sound, there is no clear path for her to stay at home full time temporarily or longer without some sort of loss.

Learned to Grieve the Loss of a Marriage

I was grieving the husband that was no longer in front of me, and I would argue I loved the persona of what he presented to me, and that was not truly him.

Betrayal is one of the hardest and most liberating things in life. They're standing right there, but they are not the person you thought you'd known. I remember crying to my therapist one time, saying it would have been more kind to have lost him with his honor intact than to accept the person standing in front of me, because all of those things I thought we shared were false.

Betrayal helps you confront and audit all the losses. This is a good thing because once you get through all the pain of realizations, then you can build a strong foundation again. Many times, we want to skip the very painful process of acceptance and clarity. Without it, we may never find our new beginning that we so desperately need, our children need, the betrayer needs, even if they don't see it at the time (repentance is key in that process), and our loved ones need, too. Then, in my journey, I realized there were so many lies that I may never know the full story, and I had to learn to let that go, as God sees it all.

A pastor said it well in his sermon about Samson: "He's a believer and self-destructs if you don't cultivate character and personal holiness." This is my situation where he is a believer yet continues to self-destruct as the character and personal holiness are nowhere to be found nor desired to be found. I would encourage you that the Bible is the lens through which we should see everything.

May I also submit that when trust is broken, it is the healthiest thing for married couples to have a year of separation. The leadership and therapists around us the first time never gave the option of a separation, based on fear. Yet, what that subjected me and our children to was an unsafe environment in every way. Spiritually, mentally, emotionally, physically, sexually. Why would you ever put an unsafe man over women and children?

This time around, the therapists were giving us the option, and we did not make it to our next session after decision night with them, as he could not keep to his word and the destruction began to fall out in a whole new way. Yet, on decision night, he immediately said yes to moving forward legally and that we would wait until the following week to get boundaries on what that would look like. Well, two days later, he already broke his word. Not surprising, but somehow a surprise to everyone else. Really?

Months later, I finally understood the cycles of abuse more clearly. I understood that good people who only interact with him in short stints cannot understand the constant double standards. Yet, my children and I are subjected to the double standard person every single day. The image keeper to the public and the Dr. Jeckel/Mr. Hyde behind closed doors.

I would like to pose these questions below to church leadership to get clarity on:

What is the biblical model of coming alongside families that are now single-parent households?

What is the role of the church in those dynamics?

From experience, I think we have to find a better marriage of taking care of those overseas and taking care of those right in our own communities as well. If we err too far in either direction, then we miss the heart of God, which is people. My hope is that any single parent, single grandparent, or person in need that is in the sphere of influence of multiple churches be accounted for and helped. What would the world look like if churches actually collaborated and used their resources in unity? Is not the Gospel of Jesus one gospel? One truth. Jesus is one way, the truth, and the life.

The church should be the first place people run to. Why? The resources and accountability go hand-in-hand, as they are right there in the community. Instead, the first place I was told to turn to and had to turn to was the government, where I became a number. I cannot see Jesus saying that to anyone. He literally met the needs of the people every single time, physically and spiritually.

Also, as a woman and truly feeling called to be home to raise my children, I for sure would argue that my presence/caretaking during crisis is needed even more and needs to be the number one option.

Why are we okay as a church or society to allow children to not only lose one parent, but then the safe parent they also lose because of money, of all things? I would propose that the safe parent can at least know that financially every six months we would reevaluate the needs and go from there.

Learned to Grieve the Loss of Motherhood

Grieving what we had agreed upon/valued—the motherhood journey for me and our children.

Motherhood is a constant joy of pivoting, problem solving, empathy, patience, energy, and so much more. My number one focus and hope was to stay home full time with my children, especially when they were young. When tragedy hits, that very value was immediately put on the chopping block because in a moment I became a single mother of two, one three-and-a-half years old and an unborn baby that would be here at any moment. May I say all these years later that God supernaturally answered that prayer every day for me to be home with my two sons even through a cross-country move, ongoing betrayal, a pandemic, multiple diseases, financial hardships, and other problems? Another miracle after miracle.

From a trauma-informed standpoint, I learned that if my safety came from "if you're pleased with me," then I am in a very unsafe environment. That dysfunctional cycle is one subjected to someone else's feelings. Feelings are subjective and not coming from our core values. If you find yourself resonating with that statement because you now realize that is your reality, then please get the professional therapeutic support to navigate healthier boundaries!

When tragedy hits a home, it ripples through every area. The notion that "these are my decisions, and it doesn't affect anyone else" is one of the greatest lies and selfish viewpoints. We are connected beings. There will always be a ripple effect, for good or evil. If no one has told you this today, I will tell you, you matter! If you're reading this, then you're alive and you have a purpose today!

You may ask, "What purpose?" I'll say put one foot in front of the other. Help someone else today. Send an encouraging text message or reel to a friend. Go to the grocery store taking carts back—just start somewhere!

Character is formed out of people who suffered. Greatness is not intelligence. Character is not formed out of being smart. *Character comes from those who suffered. Resilience comes from facing hardships and not giving up.*

Ultimately, self-control is the ultimate act of freedom. It is why it is also one of the fruits of the Spirit. Show me how you respond when the tide goes out. You will need self-control. *A lack of self-control is what put my children and me through a decade plus of consequences we did not cause.* Yet, at every crossroad, I could choose to respond rather than react. I could ask the Spirit for self-control, and He has been so faithful to give that gift freely.

Learned the Heart of the Heavenly Father

Last but definitely not least, when we grieve the living, we actually learn and get a glimpse of God's heart. Every human being on this planet is created in God's image. When Satan sees a human, he is reminded that he was kicked out of heaven for his own pride of wanting to be God. So dumb. God is God, and there will be no one else and none other.

That is why God does not wish for any man or woman to perish but to have eternal life because we literally have the

DNA of our Creator. Every person is so intricately created by God in their mother's womb. He made every human being in His image and even made the world we live in to have the very medicines, food, shelter, and other necessities to meet our needs too!

The longer I'm in this walk of life, the more I realize that our focus needs to be on Jesus and heaven. We give way too much focus to evil. When we are in alignment with Jesus and heaven, then everything in the natural realm must change.

I even ran into an older woman at the mechanic's today. We both were there to get our oil changed, and she trusted me enough to share her story. It was also one of tragedy and of single parenting, only thirty years ahead of me. I asked her," What was the most helpful thing that got you through those seasons?" Her response without batting an eye: "Pray."

PRAY before crisis, during, afterwards. PRAY. PRAY. PRAY.

This season, my prayers started off all about me and my children. Then, they changed to whatever place You walk me through, Lord, may Your presence change it for all these families and children's good. Praying for the judges to have dreams and visions. Praying for the therapist to have divine intervention and revelations.

Do not give up in doing good for in due season…

One of the prayers I've prayed over many years now is "God, give me Your eyes to see situations and people as You see them. Give me Your eyes to see me how You see me." He truly answered this prayer all these years, and it goes back to taking time to be in the secret place or purposely spending time with God each day.

SINGLE WOMAN

As a single woman, I would wake up early to pray and then at the end of the day close my day in prayer as well. On my lunch hour, going for a walk, and praying/talking to God then, too.

NEWLY MARRIED WOMAN

As a newly married woman, I would still wake up early to pray and then, at the end of the day, close my day in prayer as well.

Side note: I asked for years for my husband to pray with me, even once a week, over our tithe. It happened maybe a handful of times. Ladies, marry a disciplined man. A man with self-control. A man that gets to pray with his wife and does not scoff at the request of wanting five minutes to pray over the tithe together or at all. Red Flag!

NEW MOTHER

As a new mom, when I nursed in the night and early morning hours, that was when I would pray. I had pictures in the nursery on this wall of all those friends and family and would pray over each as I nursed. Then, all throughout the day, I took those moments for just me and Jesus, and many times my baby or toddler would be at my feet.

I can still remember I would get up in the early hours to get the baby or toddler, use the bathroom, then we would go to the downstairs family room to not wake anyone else up, and that was such a sweet time with just me and Jesus and my son or even both sons for many years.

SINGLE PARENT IN CRISIS

As a mom in crisis, I prayed when I nursed, and then I would kneel each night on the side of whatever bed I was sleeping in at night (we had many transitions) and thank God for His faithfulness each night.

MOTHER, WIFE, BUSINESS OWNER

As a mom, wife, and business owner, I prayed morning and nighttime. When I had my own soap business, many times in the studio when I poured soaps, I entered in the presence of God in that unfinished part of the basement. (Literally, my husband behind closed doors was so cruel that even when I started the soap business out of our home, he would only allow me to do it from the worst place in our home. The septic pump was there, as were all the HVAC, water pipes, and rotten shelves from the previous owner.) I did not let it stop me and cleaned that space up with the spiders, smells, and all, and God blessed it so amazingly.

Many times, this studio space is where God continued to peel back the layers of my heart, and deep healing work happened in that studio. When I was in the moment, I wondered how long, Jesus, must I endure this? And now, I miss and cherish those sweet encounters with Jesus.

A SINGLE PARENT FULLY FINANCIALLY RESPONSIBLE/ CRISIS

As a single parent, I prayed morning and nighttime, and then many times, I would call it my "Jesus drives." I know that is so corny, and I only said it to myself, but I would say, "Jesus, come join me in the van" as I would head to car lines, taking people to doctor's appointments, and so on. I had many prayerful times in bathroom stalls, on the toilet in my own home, and some of the sweetest times in His presence as I kneeled on my kitchen floor in His presence.

Fun observation: God had men go up the mountain to meet with Him in many cases. With women, God always came to them. This is just Sara's opinion here; I think it is His kindness that He meets us women wherever we are, as we are the nurturers and caregivers. That makes sense because He is love. It would not even make sense for Him to say, "Leave the baby that you just had and climb this huge mountain and wear yourself out even more or possibly fall off the side of the path." How silly! He is our vindicator, protector, strong tower. Of course, He would come to women.

As women, we go through seasons or cycles physically every month, in every way, in different stages of life. It's our superpower that I truly believe God gave women the grace and design to shoulder.

For our story, I literally had to take it one moment and one day at a time. There is no manual, nor should there be, as it is your own journey and yours alone. I still think back on our story before the affair. We were the couple that met in "sister" youth groups and were friends for a year before dating the summer before college. We took that freshman year off from dating one another, as I had moved to Washington, and he went to California for school. A year later, I transferred to California for college, and we started a friendship and dating relationship again. By the time we got married, we had dated for four years, we were engaged for a full year, and had known each other for almost five years. We got married in our home state of Maine. We went into our marriage as virgins and then moved to California to start our new life together as husband and wife. It was at year five into six when the affair happened. Our ten-year anniversary hit during the pandemic and we stayed put to celebrate. Then, in September 2021, we moved back to Maine due to an extended family medical situation. Two weeks before our cross-country move, my sister had a freak stroke and lost the whole right side of her body. It is a miracle she is still with us, and one day she will share her own story, I hope.

In these seasons of life, we have to learn to keep our focus, and sometimes that means to simply stand. It may sound simple, but it is harder than one realizes, especially when one is past their own capacity. That is the beauty of the Gospel. It is the very reason we need Jesus, as it has never been in our own strength. Our role is our willingness to remain humble. Ephesians 6:13 reminds us, "And after you have done everything, to stand."

It didn't say sit and see what happens. It didn't say go lay down in bed and sleep as much as you can to not deal with whatever situation you are facing. It said to stand. Be alert! Have your loins of truth and breastplate of righteousness. Face the situation straight on, and when it looks bleak or the chaos is still happening, don't step forward or back, but stand firm and trust God.

Story of Jehoshaphat

Stand and sing in the midst of chaos. Praise moves darkness back. Praise restored the soul because this is just Sara, but when you're downtrodden, there's not much you have left in you. But when you praise, it reminds you that God is still here! It's a new day, and I will praise because God is moving in my circumstances. That's just it. They are circumstances. It can change. Then, the Lord had the enemies turn on each other as the Israelites stood on the hill and watched it happen. God took care of it as the Israelites stood firm and praised.

There is a covenant between you and almighty God when you have given your life to Him. It was that very covenant that I reminded the Lord (not that he needed reminding), and therefore I reminded myself to hold fast to.

In the Old Testament, people would make altars or take stones and create a place of memory where they had petitioned God. Sometimes in our pain and struggles we need to physically and symbolically create those altars. Why? When it gets hard to stand firm, you can look at the altar and be encouraged because God always stays true to His promise. Notice I didn't say what we want God to do for us. But He is faithful to His Word.

November 2021

The betrayal and hurt will forever be engrained in my memory, but it doesn't have to dictate my life or the life of my family. I am trusting You, Jesus, to heal these wounds and renew my thoughts. I have been in professional ongoing therapy these past five years, and I'm so thankful I have. Take every thought captive, not just after life-transforming events but before them.

We are so quick to jump on board and focus on our faith after something has shaken our world, but where were we in our walk with Christ before our world was shaken? Whether you have been a victim in the situation or the cause, either way, the question stands. The storms of life will come. And as Christ followers, we are promised that we will have tribulations, but Jesus said, "Take heart, for I have overcome the world." For it produces perseverance. Long-suffering creates deep roots. Roots that plant us by the water. The water is the life source. Jesus is our life source. He delights in His children. If you are a Christ follower, then you are His children.

As a parent, I want to raise strong, confident sons. How they can grow and become men is by being with their parents and in a positive support system. If we aren't spending time with our Heavenly Father, then we are missing out on developing into our identity in Christ. The rest can fall away. It can all be taken away, but what is left is you. You can't get away from yourself. Sorry, but you're stuck with yourself. By God's grace, I pray your identity is in Christ and no one and nothing else. Because that's all that's left. That's all that matters and will be with you when you leave this earth. Do you know Jesus? Do you find your worth and value in Him? Whether your job is scrubbing toilets or wearing scrubs—at the end of the day, I am the Lord's! At the end of the day, have I been a good steward with what Jesus has put in front of me?

For some, it is raising the children God's given you, knowing your neighbors, fostering children, taking care of the sick, pioneering a business, reaching an unreached people group. I have to remember that at the end of my life, it is me before my Creator. Not Steve, not my bank account, or how my kids turned out. It is Sara and Jesus, and I have to give an account for my actions. I can present the opportunity to others, and however they want to participate or show up is on them. Their decisions are their own, and my response is my own.

Don't wish the days or seasons away, for they only come once. In one day, a thousand things can happen. *And it was also in one day that our Savior paid for it all.* Live and love each day to the fullest, and see God move in your life. The best place to be is in Jesus' hands, just as you are. This is the most unconditional love and gift given on this side of eternity.

CHAPTER 16
The Unknown

I wanted to write this chapter, as even in my own story and journey the end is unknown, which is one of life's greatest pleasures, frustrations, and mysteries. I am in a place where I want healthier boundaries between my spouse and me. I wish I could say that after many years of ongoing therapy for both of us, we are madly in love with one another again. However, that is not the case, as we are back in the trenches and fielding a whole new normal. I am doing the internal work with my mentor, professional therapist, close friends, and Jesus.

Remember, social media or texts show slivers of the person's journey. See and be there for one another, and do not be fooled by the "image" shown on social media. Instead of getting offended, pick up the phone and call that family member or close friend and check on them. I can say from experience that I did not forget about you. I have been in my own trenches and think about you often. In seasons like these, I longed for the days that some of you are in that seem boring or too consistent. That, my friend, is called stability. It is the greatest gift you can give your partner and yourself. Do even the small things well and consistently, and you will see the results.

I say this to myself as much as I hope to encourage you: in the beginning of this marital reconciliation, I did not know if that would truly happen, and I needed to give myself the space to let the pieces fall as they may as I kept to my own boundaries. You cannot control other people, nor did I want to. They have to want it in their own right. I needed to figure out what my own right was as well.

For me, with the type of affair and how many pieces of life it effected, mentally I had to get the foundation back to life, i.e. figure out income, housing, moving, caretaking of children and myself, meals, sleep, and all the basics of existing in this life before taking on the marital piece. Yet, Steve and I still had to "work" together to make those decisions, even with all the pain/noise going on around us. At one point, when your spouse cannot or chooses not to show up to work together, then have the courage to make the right decisions regardless. I was confident enough to make the decisions, but mentally, my marriage as I knew it just unraveled completely seconds, even minutes, ago. I was very much still coping and operating as a peacemaker. However, I can be peaceful, hold boundaries, and make decisions. It was just that now, with a huge breach of trust and not knowing how far it went, I was now the decision-maker for my family.

The Space of the In-Between

Then, when I got to Colorado, I had to get reset back up in a whole new state and then face the break in the marriage. The transition to Colorado was a shock to the system in many ways. The community support I had in California was literally life-giving. Because we were trying to leave a very unhealthy situation in California, I had a few close friends help me in Colorado, but the reality of still doing so much on my own and taking on a very broken Steve was exhausting.

    I acknowledge the trauma it has put me and my children through—the trauma it put anyone that loves or loved my little family of four through. However, I remember to hold life as an open palm. Hold out your hand for another to grab onto when they need you, or hold out your hand so others can help you as well. I am in a place in my life where I am still navigating what a healthy new normal can now look like, even five years later. I will not settle for artificial peace but hold on to the peace that rests in my heart from the Almighty, even in the present.

    A huge part of finding real peace is being informed. Each partner should know how to run the home and vice versa if, God forbid, this or something else happens to one another. *Being informed opens all forms of communication.* It uncovers any missing pieces for good or bad. On the practical side, I was informed, as I had been running our home logistically for years since Steve has a very extensive work travel schedule. Even when I would ask good questions or the right questions on the personal side, the answers I was given kept me off track and I believed him.

    Yet, how he was speaking to me unkindly did not match the words he was saying. This is a true sign of what is called gaslighting. This happens when one spouse, who is in the wrong, makes it feel like it is the other person's fault who is trying to find resolution. You are not crazy, and for over a year, I kept believing his responses, justifying it in my head, or giving the benefit of the doubt, even though behind closed doors our communication that year was so unhealthy. Once it all came to light, it made that piece of communication dysfunction clear. I was not crazy.

I was still kind in those conversations, even with being gaslit. I was being gaslit because he was hiding his adultery and wanting to continue to hide it as well. Once again, you can confront and still be kind to the other person. I wish I was more kind to myself and walked away sooner in those circular arguments because no one should be treated in that manner. No one is allowed to speak to anyone in that manner, especially if your wife is pregnant, to top it off.

A close friend of mine said way back in the waves of revelation that kept coming, the journey to reconcile may take longer and be harder than the initial break. At the time, I did not understand what that meant, and now I do. For many reasons, people are so quick to throw other people away. That is actually easier to do than to walk out a healthier new normal. *However, to get to a healthier new normal, both parties have to be willing and consistent. It cannot be one party doing things consistently and the other still being led by emotions and reactive behavior.*

Also, I pray you understand that if you are not in a healthy relationship, get the help you need. *It is not noble to enable bad behavior.* It is not being a godly wife to let your spouse continue to bring chaos into your world and your children's world. It is godlier to rebuke in love. Even with our children, we correct them because we love them. *A lack of discipline or boundaries is, in fact, a lack of love.*

In full transparency, the end of my story or the longevity of our marriage is still unknown. A healthy marriage does not equal a long marriage. There are a ton of long marriages that are anything but healthy. Give yourself the permission to realize that it is okay and may be healthier to not be married, especially for where or how the present may be.

I am not giving up giving my husband and children the family we had agreed upon long before any of this, but I also cannot continue to enable unhealthy patterns as well. Presently, I am showing up each day for myself and my family. Moving to Maine, I have a new therapist that is meeting the Sara today who has done a ton of personal work and growth. I am thankful for the mentors and therapists who have walked through so much life with me and Steve. You truly are a gift.

I pray these things may never happen to you or your family. However, life will bring many hardships, and I hope in sharing my story some piece of it can help you find clarity and peace in your own story.

Conclusion

When we grieve the living, we get a small glimpse into God's heart. The heart of God is when we see those we love standing right there in front of us, and it's not "who we once knew or remembered or want them to one day become." It truly comes down to whether we love them enough to not cross their free will. Just like our Heavenly Father loves us enough to send His Son, Jesus, so that no man would perish and have eternal life. He gives every person a choice. God does not violate our free will, and neither should we try and manipulate, convince, or coerce another person either.

If you are a Christ-follower, then I implore you to share your faith in Jesus Christ so we may no longer grieve the living people around us anymore. May we give them the chance to receive the free gift of God to all man, which is Jesus. Our responsibility is to get informed (read your Bible, get under good pastoral covering and leadership), hold clear boundaries with people, friends, and family, and present an invitation to those who are lost. Then accept that whether they want to accept or reject that invitation is their decision. It is our job to preach the saving knowledge of Jesus and the Holy Spirit's job to do the change when someone says they are willing to change.

I have said it then, and I'll say it for a lifetime: we cannot go through life without Jesus and His Holy Spirit, who is our Helper. The number one thing is to know Christ and hear His voice. He is our strength and help. Where the spirit of the Lord is, there is freedom, and all deception falls to the wayside. There will be so many decisions to make, and one final thing I have learned is it is a yes, no, or not yet response. If I did not have a clear peace on saying yes or saying no, then that meant it was a "not yet." Meaning, something else was missing or needing to pause until I got that peace, even without all the information.

Remember, the kingdom of heaven is within each and every one of us. The Holy Spirit is our Helper and is with us. The best thing we can do (for all those doers out there) is make the priority the priority, which is Jesus. He is first, whether in crisis or not. In the beginning, middle, and end. He sees it all and knew what was happening in my marriage and family way before I ever learned of it. There is nothing new under the sun, and the same answer is the same answer, Jesus. Allow Him to lead and show up in your life and your family's life. It is far better every time we take those steps of faith.

I pray if you are going through something similar today that the God of all peace will guard your heart and mind and bring you into all truth. For where the Spirit of the Lord is, there is freedom and healing. I challenge you to invite the Holy Spirit into your situation, and from that can only come freedom and healing.

www.ingramcontent.com/pod-product-compliance
Lightning Source LLC
LaVergne TN
LVHW021806160125
801488LV00005B/108